COMPETING
ON ANALYTICS

COMPETING ON ANALYTICS

The New Science of Winning

THOMAS H. DAVENPORT
and JEANNE G. HARRIS

HARVARD BUSINESS SCHOOL PRESS
BOSTON, MASSSACHUSETTS

Copyright 2007 Harvard Business School Publishing Corporation
All rights reserved
Printed in the United States of America

12 11 10   15

No part of this publication may be reproduced, stored in or introduced into a retrieval
system, or transmitted, in any form, or by any means (electronic, mechanical,
photocopying, recording, or otherwise), without the prior permission of the publisher.
Requests for permission should be directed to permissions@hbsp.harvard.edu, or
mailed to Permissions, Harvard Business School Publishing, 60 Harvard Way, Boston,
Massachusetts 02163.

Library of Congress Cataloging-in-Publication Data
Davenport, Thomas H., 1954–
    Competing on analytics : the new science of winning / Thomas H.
Davenport and Jeanne G. Harris.
        p. cm.
    ISBN-13: 978-1-4221-0332-6 (hardcover : alk. paper)
    1. Business mathematics. 2. Business intelligence. I. Harris, Jeanne
    G. II. Title.
HF5691.D38 2007
658.4'013—dc22   2006035422

The paper used in this publication meets the requirements of the American National
Standard for Permanence of Paper for Publications and Documents in Libraries and
Archives Z39.48-1992.

To Helen, with thanks for Jodi and much more

—Tom

To Carl and Lauren

—Jeanne

Contents

Part Two
Building an Analytical Capability

Foreword

WHEN I WAS A DOCTORAL student in economics at the Massachusetts Institute of Technology, a powerful theory known as *rational expectations* suggested that it was difficult to profit from widely anticipated, or predictable, events, since rational actors would already have taken the action necessary to arbitrage any such opportunities. When I became a student of management, I assumed that an extension of rational expectations would apply in business; that is, any straightforward profit-enhancing opportunity in competitive markets would already be exploited and hence unavailable at the margin.

Well, thank goodness for me and the shareholders of Harrah's Entertainment, Inc. that rational expectations is a far from complete characterization of managerial behavior. In short, opportunities abound to employ simple analytic methods to marginally or substantially increase profitability, especially in large businesses such as mine where a single insight can ring the cash register literally thousands or millions of times. Examples abound in casino resort entertainment, including yield management, game pricing, customer relationship management, loyalty programs, and procurement. To take perhaps the easiest and biggest opportunity in my tenure, we found that a ten-basis-point movement of slot pricing toward the estimated demand curve for a given game could enhance our profitability by an eight-figure amount and be unobservable to the guest.

The fact that this slot-pricing opportunity was available for someone as simple minded as myself to find and exploit illustrates several of the common impediments to analytic management that have absolutely nothing to do with either analytic methods, data availability, or technology.

As Davenport and Harris demonstrate elegantly in this important and unprecedented deep dive on the subject, analytic management is impeded by common organizational pathologies:

- A powerful conventional wisdom, often associated with powerful people, is allowed to sustain itself absent critical testing.

- Decision making, especially at high levels, not only fails to demand rigor and dispassionate analysis, but often champions the opposite as the scarce talent that identifies CEOs and visionaries from otherwise smart but less inspired people.

- The organization lacks people who get up in the morning eager to do analytic empirical work and are really good at it. Instead, analytic work is seen as the last resort, undertaken by those unfamiliar with proper methods.

- People tend to win over ideas rather than the reverse.

Indulge me a few words about each of these culprits, beginning with the last. The owners of any company, especially mine, deserve the very best ideas to be put into practice. While I hope Harrah's Entertainment shareholders have some confidence in me, they are far better served to have confidence in the capability of my team to gather and test the best ideas available within and outside of Harrah's Entertainment and use only those that lead to sustained superior performance and growth. Although God has graced me with one or two respectable ideas, she has also saddled me with some real losers and a frequent state of ignorance and confusion. It is not my job to have all the answers, but it is my job to ask lots of penetrating, disturbing and occasionally almost offensive questions as part of the analytic process that leads to insight and refinement.

My journey is complicated by the fact that all organizations seek to please the leader, so there is constant pressure to give my otherwise lame and ill-considered views far more gravitas than they deserve. Beware, as this process can feel good and be dangerously addictive. Indeed, conventional wisdoms are often birthed in just this way. Hence, it is critical to create and constantly cultivate an environment that views ideas as separable from people, insists on the use of rigorous evidence to distinguish among ideas, and includes a healthy dose of people both sufficiently dedicated and skillful to do the heavy lifting. Davenport and Harris have provided the guide for creating such an environment, informed by best practice from a heterogeneous group of innovative organizations.

One last thing. When it comes to visionary leadership as compared to analytic management, you can lose weight without diet or exercise. Or to put it differently, vision and analytics need not be seen as mutually exclusive paradigms. In my industry, Steve Wynn and Jack Binion have both been visionary leaders of great accomplishment. Neither were students of traditional analytic methods, but both were innovators whose ideas were entirely consistent with analytic methods. The challenge for those of us who attempt to employ analytic capabilities is to ensure that they are oriented forward, where the problems are least well defined and the data is scarce, rather than backward, where the work is easy and the risk is low. Read ahead. There is much to learn.

Gary Loveman
Chairman of the Board, President,
and Chief Executive Officer
Harrah's Entertainment, Inc.

Acknowledgments

THIS BOOK BEGAN WITH A phone call to Tom. Scott Van Valkenburgh, head of platform partner relationships at the business intelligence software firm SAS Institute, called me (after being directed to me by Keri Pearlson of The Concours Group—thanks, Keri) and asked me if I was interested in doing some research on the state of business intelligence in companies. I quickly said, "Heck yes," because my former colleague at Accenture Jeanne Harris and I had done some previous research in that domain, and I was still very interested in it. Scott brought his colleague Mike Bright and a couple of his partners from Intel up for a meeting at Babson, and we embarked upon the research that led to this book. Thanks to Scott, Mike, Jim Davis, Margo Stutesman, Keith Collins, and Jim Watts at SAS, and Andy Fields and his colleagues and predecessors at Intel for getting us started on the "competing on analytics" idea and providing numerous insights along the way.

In January 2006 I wrote a *Harvard Business Review* article on the subject—thanks to Leigh Buchanan for doing a great job of editing it and pushing my thinking—and it took off better than just about anything I've written. I did some further research sponsored by my friends at SAP—thanks to Dan Pantaleo and Stacy Comes of the Strategic Issues Group there, and Roman Bukary, who headed the BI practice at the time. Things were going so well that I decided to explore a book on the topic. I knew that Jeanne Harris had once led the business intelligence practice at Accenture, and was a great coauthor. We approached my old friends at Harvard Business School Press—thanks to Hollis Heimbouch and Astrid Sandoval for saying "go for it" and being great editors. Their colleagues in the conferences side of HBS Publishing, Eric McNulty and

Angelia Herrin, worked with SAS and Intel to put on a great conference on the subject in New York. Thanks to them too. Now nothing was left but the writing. I'll let Jeanne talk about who helped on her side.

I want to begin by expressing my deepest thanks to the many senior executives at Accenture who have shared their enthusiastic support and encouragement along the way. Our CEO Bill Green said he thought the book was a great idea. Particular thanks go to Bob Thomas, executive director of the Institute for High-Performance Business, and Tim Breene, who heads Accenture's strategy and corporate development, for their consistent support and always incisive insights. With their encouragement, I enlisted many smart, prominent senior executives at Accenture who willingly shared their firsthand experience and expertise working with clients to compete (and win) with analytics. Thanks especially go to our research sponsors for their support and honest feedback: Mike Sutcliff, Managing Director for New Businesses; Royce Bell, CEO of Accenture Information Management Solutions; Alton Adams of our Customer Relationship Management practice; Hettie Tabor, who leads the SAP business intelligence consulting; and David Mann, a leader in our Products practice. Thank you also to the sponsors of the enterprise systems and analytics survey: Dave Hill, Patrick Puechbroussou, Jim Hayes, and Mark Jones.

In addition to contributing their insights, many Accenture senior executives helped me find some outstanding examples to showcase in the book, including Walt Shill, Paul Nunes, Brian McCarthy, Jeff Merrihue, Umesh Hari, Jane Linder, John Copeland, Ramin Mikhali, David Sheehy, Sanjay Mathur, Baiju Shah, Andy Fano, and John Ballow. I am, as always, grateful to my friends and colleagues at the Accenture Institute for High Performance Business for their generous assistance and willingness to contribute great ideas. Finally, I want to express special thanks to Pete Bott, Norm Rickeman, and Jean Davis, who many years ago set me on the path that eventually led to writing this book.

Of course, we (Jeanne and Tom) reserve our greatest thanks for the pioneering executives of analytical competitors who freely gave of their time. We interviewed lots of them, but the earliest and most generous contributors (more or less in sequence) were Gary Loveman and David Norton of Harrah's, Glen Wegryn of Procter & Gamble, Zahir Balaporia of Schneider National, Inc., Ed Ng of Mars, Nell Williams and Stefan Chase of Marriott International, Gregor Bailar of Capital One Financial

Corporation, Bubba Tyler of Quaker Chemical Corporation (now at IMS Health), Kent Kushar of E. & J. Gallo, Steve Schmidt of Vertex Pharmaceuticals, Inc., and Jeff Zabin at Fair Isaac Corporation.

For help in doing the research, editing, and pumping out the prose, we'd like to thank Mike Beers, Don Cohen, Linda Harding, Al Jacobson, Christine Lentz, David Light, Chi Pham, Erica Toomey, and especially Eric Lowitt. Thanks also to five anonymous reviewers, one of whom we're pretty sure included our diligent and wise friend and former colleague Mark McDonald. We did our best to take your counsel to heart and hope you like the results.

We'd also like to thank our families for dealing with our first (Jeanne) and twelfth (Tom) books, respectively. Jeanne especially thanks her husband Carl and her daughter Lauren for their love, encouragement, and inspiration. She could not have completed this book without them; together they give her life meaning and much happiness. She also thanks her mother Rhoda Harris and sister Susie for their unwavering encouragement and enthusiasm. Tom thanks Jodi for predicting that the analytics topic would be a hot one and for once again enthusiastically supporting his every venture. He's analyzed all his personal data and discovered that his wife is highly correlated with his happiness. He thanks his sons Hayes and Chase for passionate discussions about baseball as an analytical discipline, particularly the Boston Red Sox.

Part One

The Nature of Analytical Competition

I

The Nature of Analytical Competition

Using Analytics to Build a Distinctive Capability

In 1997, a thirty-something man whose resume included software geek, education reformer, and movie buff rented *Apollo 13* from the biggest video-rental chain on the block—Blockbuster—and got hit with $40 in late fees. That dent in his wallet got him thinking: why didn't video stores work like health clubs, where you paid a flat monthly fee to use the gym as much as you wanted? Because of this experience—and armed with the $750 million he received for selling his software company—Reed Hastings jumped into the frothy sea of the "new economy" and started Netflix, Inc.

Pure folly, right? After all, Blockbuster was already drawing in revenues of more than $3 billion per year from its thousands of stores across America and in many other countries—and it wasn't the only competitor in this space. Would people really order their movies online, wait for the U.S. Postal Service (increasingly being referred to as "snail mail" by the late 1990s) to deliver them, and then go back to the mailbox to return the films? Surely Netflix would go the route of the many Net-based companies that had a "business model" and a marketing pitch but no customers.

And yet we know that the story turned out differently, and a significant reason for Netflix's success today is that it is an analytical competitor. The movie delivery company, which has grown from $5 million in revenues in 1999 to about $1 billion in 2006, is a prominent example of a firm that competes on the basis of its mathematical, statistical, and data management prowess. Netflix offers free shipping of DVDs to its roughly 6 million customers and provides a return shipping package, also free. Customers watch their cinematic choices at their leisure; there are no late fees. When the DVDs are returned, customers select their next films.

Besides the logistical expertise that Netflix needs to make this a profitable venture, Netflix employs analytics in two important ways, both driven by customer behavior and buying patterns. The first is a movie-recommendation "engine" called Cinematch that's based on proprietary, algorithmically driven software. Netflix hired mathematicians with programming experience to write the algorithms and code to define clusters of movies, connect customer movie rankings to the clusters, evaluate thousands of ratings per second, and factor in current Web site behavior—all to ensure a personalized Web page for each visiting customer.

Netflix has also created a $1 million prize for quanitative analysts outside the company who can improve the cinematch algorithm by at least 10 percent. Netflix CEO Reed Hastings notes, "If the Starbucks secret is a smile when you get your latte, ours is that the Web site adapts to the individual's taste."[1] Netflix analyzes customers' choices and customer feedback on the movies they have rented—over 1 billion reviews of movies they liked, loved, hated, and so forth—and recommends movies in a way that optimizes both the customer's taste and inventory conditions. Netflix will often recommend movies that fit the customer's preference profile but that aren't in high demand. In other words, its primary territory is in "the long tail—the outer limits of the normal curve where the most popular products and offerings don't reside."[2]

Netflix also engages in a somewhat controversial, analytically driven practice called *throttling*. Throttling refers to how the company balances the distribution of shipping requests across frequent-use and infrequent-use customers. Infrequent-use customers are given priority in shipping over frequent-use customers. There are multiple reasons for this practice. Because shipping is free to customers and the monthly charge to the customer is fixed, infrequent-use customers are the most profitable to Netflix. Like all companies, Netflix wants to keep its most profitable customers satisfied and prevent them from leaving. And while frequent-use customers may feel they are being treated unfairly (there have been complaints by a small number of customers, according to Hastings), Netflix must distribute its shipping resources across its most and least profitable customers in a way that makes economic sense. Hastings refers to the practice as a *fairness algorithm*. Netflix recently settled a class action suit involving the practice, because it had advertised that most movies were shipped in a day.

Analytics also help Netflix decide what to pay for the distribution rights to DVDs. When the company bought the rights to *Favela Rising*, a documentary about musicians in Rio de Janeiro slums, Netflix executives were aware that a million customers had ordered from the company the 2003 movie *City of God*, a realistic drama set in the slums of Rio. It also knew that 500,000 customers had selected a somewhat related documentary about slum life in India, *Born into Brothels*, and 250,000 ordered both DVDs from Netflix. Therefore, the company's buyers felt safe in paying for 250,000 rentals. If more are ordered, both *Favela Rising's* producers and Netflix benefit.

Like most analytical competitors, Netflix has a strong culture of analytics and a "test and learn" approach to its business. The chief product officer, Neil Hunt, notes,

> From product management all the way down to the engineering team, we have hired for and have built a culture of quantitative tests. We typically have several hundred variations of consumer experience experiments running at once. For example, right now we're trying out the "Netflix Screening Room," which lets customers see previews of movies they haven't seen. We have built four different versions of that for the test. We put 20,000 subscribers into each of four test cells, and we have a control group that doesn't get the screening room at all. We measure how long they spend viewing previews, what the completion rate is, how many movies they add to their queue, how it affects ratings of movies they eventually order, and a variety of other factors. The initial data is quite promising.

Netflix's CEO, Hastings, has a master's in computer science from Stanford and is a former Peace Corps math teacher. The company has introduced science into a notably artistic industry. As a *Business Week* article put it, "Netflix uses data to make decisions moguls make by gut. The average user rates more than 200 films, and Netflix crunches consumers' rental history and film ratings to predict what they'll like . . . 'It's *Moneyball* for movies [referring to the Oakland Athletics' usage of statistics in professional baseball], with geeks like Reed looking at movies as just another data problem,' says Netflix board member Richard N. Barton."

In its testing, Netflix employs a wide variety of quantitative and qualitative approaches, including primary surveys, Web site user testing, concept development and testing, advertising testing, data mining, brand awareness studies, subscriber satisfaction, channel analysis, marketing mix optimization, segmentation research, and marketing material effectiveness. The testing pervades the culture and extends from marketing to operations to customer service.

The company's analytical orientation has already led to a high level of success and growth. But the company is also counting on analytics to drive it through a major technological shift. It's already clear that the distribution of movies will eventually move to electronic channels—the Internet, cable, or over the air. The exact mix and timing aren't clear, but the long-term future of the mailed DVD isn't bright. Netflix, however, is counting on its analytics to help it prosper in a virtual distribution world. If Netflix knows more than anyone else about what movies its customers want to see, the logic goes, customers will stay with the company no matter how the movies get to their screens.

Netflix may seem unique, but in many ways it is typical of the companies and organizations—a small but rapidly growing number of them—that have recognized the potential of business analytics and have aggressively moved to realize it. They can be found in a variety of industries (see figure 1-1). Some, like Netflix, are not widely known as analytical competitors. Others, like Harrah's Entertainment in the gaming industry or the Oakland A's in baseball, have already been celebrated in books and articles. Some, such as Amazon.com, Yahoo!, and Google, are recent start-ups that have harnessed the power of the Internet to their analytical engines. Others, such as Mars and Procter & Gamble, have made familiar consumer goods for a century or more. These companies have only two things in common: they compete on the basis of their analytical capabilities, and they are highly successful in their industries. These two attributes, we believe, are not unrelated.

FIGURE 1-1

Analytic competitors are found in a variety of industries

Consumer products
- Anheuser-Busch
- E. & J. Gallo Winery
- Mars
- Procter & Gamble

Financial services
- Barclays Bank
- Capital One
- Royal Bank of Canada
- Progressive Casualty Insurance
- WellPoint

Hospitality and entertainment
- Oakland A's
- Boston Red Sox
- Harrah's Entertainment
- Marriott International
- New England Patriots

Industrial products
- CEMEX
- John Deere & Company

Pharmaceuticals
- AstraZeneca
- Solvay
- Vertex Pharmaceuticals, Inc.

Retail
- Amazon.com
- JCPenny
- Tesco
- Wal-Mart

Telecommunications
- Sprint
- O2
- Bouygues Telecom

Transport
- FedEx
- Schneider National
- United Parcel Service

eCommerce
- Google
- Netflix, Inc.
- Yahoo!

What Are Analytics?

By *analytics* we mean the extensive use of data, statistical and quantitative analysis, explanatory and predictive models, and fact-based management to drive decisions and actions. The analytics may be input for human decisions or may drive fully automated decisions. Analytics are a subset of what has come to be called *business intelligence*: a set of technologies and processes that use data to understand and analyze business performance. As figure 1-2 suggests, business intelligence includes both data access and reporting, and analytics. Each of these approaches addresses a range of questions about an organization's business activities. The questions that analytics can answer represent the higher-value and more proactive end of this spectrum.

In principle, analytics could be performed using paper, pencil, and perhaps a slide rule, but any sane person using analytics today would employ information technology. The range of analytical software goes from relatively simple statistical and optimization tools in spreadsheets (Excel being the primary example, of course), to statistical software packages (e.g., Minitab), to complex business intelligence suites (SAS,

FIGURE 1-2

Business intelligence and analytics

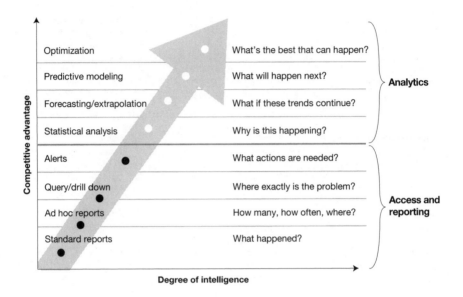

Source: Adapted from a graphic produced by SAS. Used with permission.

Cognos, BusinessObjects), predictive industry applications (Fair Isaac), and the reporting and analytical modules of major enterprise systems (SAP and Oracle). And as we'll describe later in the book, good analytical capabilities also require good information management capabilities to integrate, extract, transform, and access business transaction data. Some people, then, would simply equate analytics with analytical information technology. But this would be a huge mistake—as we'll argue throughout this book, it's the human and organizational aspects of analytical competition that are truly differentiating.

Why Compete on Analytics?

At a time when companies in many industries offer similar products and use comparable technology, high-performance business processes are among the last remaining points of differentiation. Many of the previous bases for competition are no longer available. Unique geographical advantage doesn't matter in global competition, and protective regulation is largely gone. Proprietary technologies are rapidly copied, and breakthrough innovation in products or services seems increasingly difficult to achieve. What's left as a basis for competition is to execute your business with maximum efficiency and effectiveness, and to make the smartest business decisions possible. And analytical competitors wring every last drop of value from business processes and key decisions.

Analytics can support almost any business process. Yet organizations that want to be competitive must have some attribute at which they are better than anyone else in their industry—a distinctive capability.[3] This usually involves some sort of business process or some type of decision. Maybe you strive to make money by being better at identifying profitable and loyal customers than your competition, and charging them the optimal price for your product or service. If so, analytics are probably the answer to being the best at it. Perhaps you sell commodity products and need to have the lowest possible level of inventory while preventing your customer from being unable to find your product on the shelf; if so, analytics are often the key to supply chain optimization. Perhaps you compete in a people-intensive business and are seeking to hire, retain, and promote the best people in the industry. There too, analytics can be the key (though thus far they have largely been used for this purpose in professional sports and not much in businesses).

On the other hand, perhaps your operational business processes aren't much different from anybody else's, but you feel you compete on making the best decisions. Maybe you can choose the best locations for your stores—if so, you're probably doing it analytically. You may build scale through mergers and acquisitions, and select only the best candidates for such combinations. Most don't work out well, according to widely publicized research, but yours do. If so, you're probably not making those decisions primarily on intuition. Good decisions usually have systematically assembled data and analysis behind them.

Analytical competitors, then, are organizations that have selected one or a few distinctive capabilities on which to base their strategies, and then have applied extensive data, statistical and quantitative analysis, and fact-based decision making to support the selected capabilities. Analytics themselves don't constitute a strategy, but using them to optimize a distinctive business capability certainly constitutes a strategy. Whatever the capabilities emphasized in a strategy, analytics can propel them to a higher level. Capital One, for example, calls its approach to analytical competition "information-based strategy." Harrah's distinctive capabilities are customer loyalty and service, and it has certainly optimized them with its analytically driven strategy.

Can any organization in any industry successfully compete on analytics? This is an interesting question that we've debated between ourselves. On the one hand, virtually any business would seem to have the potential for analytical competition. The cement business, for example, would seem to be as prosaic and nonanalytical an industry as one could find. But the global cement giant CEMEX has successfully applied analytics to its distinctive capability of optimized supply chains and delivery times.

On the other hand, some industries are clearly more amenable to analytics than others. If your business generates lots of transaction data—such as in financial services, travel and transportation, or gaming—competing on analytics is a natural strategy (though many firms still don't do it). If your business model is based on hard-to-measure factors—like style, as in the fashion business, or human relationships, as in the executive search industry—it would take much more groundbreaking work to compete on analytics. Still, virtually every day we find examples of businesses that were previously intuitive but are now becoming analytical. The wine business, for example, was once and (in some quarters) still is highly intuitive and built on unpredictable consumer preferences. Today, however, it's possible to quantitatively analyze and predict the appeal of any wine, and large winemakers such as E. & J. Gallo are competing on analytics in such domains as sales, agriculture, and understanding of consumer preferences.[4]

How This Book Can Help

We didn't invent the idea of competing on analytics, but we believe that this book (and the articles we wrote that preceded it) are the first to describe the phenomenon.[5] In this book, you'll find more on the topic than has ever been compiled: more discussion of the concept, more examples of organizations that are pursuing analytical competition, more management issues to be addressed, and more specific applications of analytics. Part I of the book lays out the definition and key attributes of analytical competition, and discusses (with some analytics!) how it can lead to better business performance. The end of this part describes a variety of applications of competitive analytics, first internally and then externally, with customers and suppliers.

Part II of the book is more of a how-to guide. It begins with an overall road map for organizations wishing to compete on their analytical capabilities. Whole chapters are devoted to each of the two key resources—human and technological—needed to make this form of competition a reality. We conclude by discussing some of the key directions for business analytics in the future.

There are a lot of words here, but we know they won't be the last on the topic. We know of several other authors planning books on it, and we hope there will be a raft of articles too. We hope that many academics and consultants will embrace the topic. If this field is to prosper, the world will have to spend a lot of time and energy focusing on it, and we'll need all the guidance we can get.

How Did We Get Here?
The Origins of Analytical Competition

The planets are clearly aligned for the move to analytical competition by organizations. At the same time that executives have been looking for new sources of advantage and differentiation, they have more data about their businesses than ever before. Enterprise resource planning (ERP) systems, point-of-sale (POS) systems, and Web sites, among other sources, have created more and better transaction data than in the history of humankind. A new generation of technically literate executives—the first to grow up with computers—is coming into organizations and looking for new ways to manage them with the help of technology. Finally, the ability to make sense of data through computers and software has finally come of age. Analytical software makers have dramatically expanded the functionality of their products over the past several years, and hardware providers have optimized their technologies for fast analysis and the management of large databases.

The use of analytics began as a small, out-of-the-way activity performed in a few data-intensive business functions. As early as the late 1960s, practitioners and researchers began to experiment with the use of computer systems to analyze data and support decision making. Called *decision support systems* (DSS), these applications were used for analytical, repetitive, and somewhat narrow activities such as production planning, investment portfolio management, and transportation routing. Two DSS pioneers, Peter Keen and Charles Stabell, argue that the concept of decision support arose from studies of organizational decision making done at Carnegie Tech (now Carnegie Mellon) by researchers such as Herbert Simon during the late 1950s and early '60s, and technical work on interactive computer systems, mainly carried out at MIT in the 1960s.[6] Others would argue that their origins were closely connected to military applications in and following World War II, although computers as we know them were not yet available for those applications.

Statistical analysis on computers became a much more mainstream activity in the 1970s, as companies such as SAS Institute and SPSS introduced packaged computer applications that made statistics accessible to many researchers and businesspeople. Yet despite the greater availability of statistics, DSS did not prosper in the period and evolved into *executive support systems*.[7] These applications involved direct use of computers and data by senior executives for monitoring and reporting of performance (with a lesser emphasis on decision making). This activity also never took off broadly, in part because of the reluctance of executives to engage in hands-on use.

Analytical technology became most frequently used for storing relatively small amounts of data and conducting ad hoc queries in support of decisions and performance monitoring. The focus on managing data became important because vast amounts of it were becoming available from transaction systems such as ERP and POS systems, and later from Internet transactions. Versions of this data-oriented focus were referred to as OLAP (online analytical processing) and later *data warehousing*. Smaller data warehouses were called *data marts*.

Today, as we mentioned, the entire field is often referred to with the term *business intelligence* and incorporates the collection, management, and reporting of decision-oriented data as well as the analytical techniques and computing approaches that are performed on the data. Business intelligence overall is a broad and popular field within the IT industry—in fact, a 2006 Gartner survey of 1,400 chief information officers suggests that business intelligence is the number one technology priority for IT organizations.[8] Two studies of large organizations using ERP systems that we did in 2002 and 2006 revealed that better decision making was the primary benefit sought, and (in 2006) analytics were the technology most sought to take advantage of the ERP data.

Despite the variation in terminology, these movements—each of which lasted about a decade—had several attributes in common. They were largely technically focused, addressing how computers could be used to store, analyze, and display data and results of analysis. They were focused on fairly narrow problems—with the exception of the executive and performance monitoring systems, which only displayed the condition of the business. They were also relegated to the "back office" of organizations—used by technicians and specialists, with little visibility to senior executives. With only a few exceptions, they could rarely be said to influence the nature of competition.

Today, most large organizations have some sort of analytical applications in place and some business intelligence tools installed. But they are typically marginal to the success of the business and are managed at the departmental level. An insurance company, for example, may have some analytical tools and approaches in the actuarial department, where pricing for policies is determined. A manufacturing company may use such tools for quality management. Marketing may have some capabilities for lifetime value analysis for customers. However valuable these activities are, they are invisible to senior executives, customers, and shareholders—and they can't be said to drive the company's competitive strategy. They are important to individual functions but insignificant to competition overall.

Our focus in this book, however, is on companies that have elevated data management, statistical and quantitative analysis, and fact-based decision making to a high art. These organizations have analytical activities that are hardly invisible; they are touted to every stakeholder and interested party by CEOs. Rather than being in the back room, analytics in these companies are found in the annual report and in the press clippings. These organizations have taken a resource that is ostensibly available to all, and refined it to such a degree that their strategies are built around it.

When Are Analytical Decisions Appropriate?

There is considerable evidence that decisions based on analytics are more likely to be correct than those based on intuition.[9] It's better to know—at least within the limits of data and analysis—than to believe or think or feel, and most companies can benefit from more analytical decision making. Of course, there are some circumstances in which decisions can't or shouldn't be based on analytics. Some of these circumstances are described in Malcolm Gladwell's popular book *Blink*, which is a paean to intuitive decision making.[10] It's ironic that a book praising intuition would arise and become popular just when many organizations are relying heavily on analytics, but then perhaps that's part of its romantic appeal. The book is fun and persuasive, but it doesn't make clear that intuition is only appropriate under certain circumstances. Gladwell is undoubtedly correct, for example, that human beings evolved a capability to make accurate and quick decisions about each other's personality and intentions, and it's rare for formal analysis to do that as well. Yet even Gladwell argues that intuition is a good guide to action only when it's backed by many years of expertise. And many of Gladwell's examples of intuition are only possible because of years of analytical research in the background, such as Dr. John Gottsman's rapid and seemingly intuitive judgments of whether a married couple he observes will stay together. He's only able to make such assessments because he observed and statistically analyzed thousands of hours of videotaped interactions by couples.

It's also clear that decision makers have to use intuition when they have no data and must make a very rapid decision—as in Gladwell's example of police officers deciding whether to shoot a suspect. Gary Klein, a consultant on decision making, makes similar arguments about firefighters making decisions about burning buildings.[11] Even firms that are generally quite analytical must sometimes resort to intuition when they have no data. For example, Jeff Bezos, CEO of Amazon.com, greatly prefers to perform limited tests of new features on Amazon.com, rigorously quantifying user reaction before rolling them out. But the company's "search inside the book" offering was impossible to test without applying it to a critical mass of books (Amazon.com started with 120,000). It was also expensive to develop, increasing the risk. In that case, Bezos trusted his instincts and took a flier. And the feature did prove popular when introduced.[12]

Of course, any quantitative analysis relies upon a series of assumptions. When the conditions behind the assumptions no longer apply, the analyses should no longer be employed. For example, Capital One and other credit card companies make analytical predictions about customers' willingness to repay their balances under conditions of general economic prosperity. If the economy took a sharp downturn, the predictions would no longer apply, and it would be dangerous to continue using them.

The key message is that the frontier of decisions that can be treated analytically is always moving forward. Areas of decision making that were once well suited for intuition accumulate data and analytical rigor over time, and intuition becomes suboptimal. Today, for example, some executives still consider it feasible to make major decisions about mergers and acquisitions from their gut. However, the best firms are already using detailed analytics to explore such decisions. Procter & Gamble, for example, used a variety of analytical techniques before its acquisition of Gillette, including those for logistics and supply chains, drivers of stock market value, and human resources. In a few years, firms that do not employ extensive analytics in making a major acquisition will be considered irresponsible.

Indeed, trends point to a more analytical future for virtually every firm. The amount of data available will only continue to increase. Radio frequency identification (RFID) devices will be put on virtually every pallet or carton that moves through the supply chain, generating vast amounts of new data for companies to collect and analyze. In retail, every shopping cart will be intelligent enough to gather data on "pick-streams," or a record of which products are taken off the shelves in what order. In oil exploration and mining, the amount of data—already massive—will expand geometrically. In advertising, more businesses are already shifting to media such as the Internet and cable television that can monitor which ads are seen by whom—again creating a huge new stream of data.

Analytical software will become more broadly available and will be in reach of every organization. Statistically oriented software firms such as SAS and SPSS have made increasingly sophisticated analyses available to average companies and users for over thirty years, and they will continue to do so. Business intelligence firms such as SAS, Business Objects, and Cognos are adding more analytical capabilities to their software toolsets. New industry applications targeting different business capabilities will become available from vendors such as Fair Isaac Corporation. Enterprise systems vendors such as SAP and Oracle are making it more possible to analyze their systems' data and monitor the performance of the business. And Microsoft is incorporating increasing amounts of analytical capability into basic office software. In the future, software availability will not be an issue in analytical competition, although the ability to use analytical software well won't ever be a commodity.

It's also safe to assume that hardware won't be a problem. Today the 64-bit processors from Intel and others that can do extensive quantitative analysis on large data sets are considered cutting-edge, but they won't be for long. Specialized computers from providers such as Teradata and Netezza can easily manage multiterabyte data warehouses. No doubt the personal computer of the near future will be able to perform serious analyses. The bigger issue will be how organizations control their data and analysis, and ensure that individual users make decisions on correct analyses and assumptions.

To remain an analytical competitor, however, means staying on the leading edge. Analytical competition will be something of an arms race, requiring continual development of new measures, new algorithms, and new decision-making approaches. Firms embracing it will systematically eliminate guesswork from their processes and business models. Analytical competitors will have to conduct experiments in many aspects of their businesses and learn from each one of them. In order for quantitative decisions to be implemented effectively, analysis will have to be a broad capability of employees, rather than the province of a few "rocket scientists" with quantitative expertise.

We've developed a road map describing the primary steps needed to build an effective analytical competitor. It involves key prerequisites, such as having at least a moderate amount and quality of data about the domain of business that analytics will support, and having the right types of hardware and software on hand. The key variables are human, however. One prerequisite is that some manager must have enough commitment to analytics to develop the idea further. But then the pivotal factor in how fast and how well an organization proceeds along the analytical path is sponsorship. Firms such as Netflix, Harrah's, and Capital One have CEO-level sponsorship and even passion for analytical competition that lets them proceed on a "full steam ahead" path.

Other organizations that lack passionate executive sponsorship must first go through a "prove it" path to demonstrate the value of analytical competition. This path is slower, and even those who take the prove-it path have to eventually arrive at strong executive sponsorship if they are to become true analytical competitors. We will discuss this road map—and the steps on each of the two paths—in greater detail in the second part of this book (chapter 6 in particular). For now, we simply want to emphasize that although analytics seem to be dispassionate and computer based, the most important factors leading to success involve passionate people.

Analytics in Professional Sports—and Their Implications for Business

We can perhaps best understand the progression of analytical competition across an industry by focusing on professional sports. While sports differ, of course, they have in common large amounts of data and talented but expensive human resources (the athletes). Sports also differ from businesses, but both domains of activity have in common the need to optimize critical resources and of course the need to win.

Perhaps the most analytical professional sport is baseball, which has long been the province of quantitative and statistical analysis. The use of statistics and new measures in baseball received considerable visibility with the publication of *Moneyball*, by Michael Lewis.[13] The book described the analytical orientation of the Oakland A's, a professional team that had a record of consistently making the playoffs despite a low overall payroll (including the 2006 playoffs—although, even the best analytical competitor doesn't win all the time, as in 2005). Lewis described the conversion of Oakland's general manager (GM), Billy Beane, to analytics for player selection when he realized that he himself had possessed all the traditional attributes of a great player, according to major league scouts. Yet Beane had not been a great player, so he began to focus more on actual player performance as revealed in statistics than on the potential to be great. Beane and the A's also began to make use of relatively new measures of player performance, eschewing the traditional "runs batted in," or RBIs, and focusing on "on-base percentage" and "on-base plus slugging percentage." Like analytical competitors in business, they invented new metrics that assessed and stretched their performance.

Yet Beane was not actually the first Oakland general manager to take a statistical orientation.[14] In the early 1980s, Sandy Alderson, then the GM (now CEO of the San Diego Padres, another 2006 playoff contender), adopted a more statistical approach for two reasons. First, Oakland had performed badly for a number of years before the decision and was on the brink of going out of business. Second, Alderson was offered an early version of a PC-based (actually, Apple II–based) statistical database and analysis package. Baseball statistics are widely available from firms such as STATS, Inc., and the Elias Sports Bureau, although the statistics were available to teams well before they started taking advantage of them. These reasons are typical of why businesses often adopt analytical competition: a combination of pressing business need, the availability of data, and IT that can crunch all the numbers.

The analytical approach to baseball has broadened considerably over the last few years. One team that has adopted the "moneyball" approach is the Boston Red Sox—a team with both analytical capabilities and the money to invest in expensive players. The Red Sox also had a business need, having failed to win the World Series for eighty-six years by the 2004 season. The Sox also exemplify another reason why organizations adopt analytical competition: new leadership. The team's two new principal owners in 2002 were John Henry, a quantitative hedge fund manager, and Tom Werner, a television producer who had previously owned the San Diego Padres. The appeal of analytics to Henry was obvious, but Werner had also realized with the Padres that the traditional baseball establishment didn't know as much about what led to championships as it purported to. As we mentioned earlier, the high level of executive sponsorship at the Sox let the team take the full-steam-ahead approach to analytical competition.

Like other organizations committed to analytical strategies, the Red Sox quickly hired as a consultant the best analytical talent: Bill James, who was widely regarded as the world's foremost practitioner of "sabermetrics," or baseball statistics (James even invented the term himself). The fact that no other team had seen fit to hire such an underemployed analytical genius suggests that analytical competition in baseball was not yet widespread. The analytical approach—along with some new and expensive talent—paid off for the Sox quickly, and they made the American League Championship Series (ALCS) against their perennial rivals, the New York Yankees, in 2003.

Yet one game in that series illustrates a key difficulty of analytical competition: it has to spread everywhere within an organization if analytical decisions are to be implemented. In the fifth and deciding game of the series, Red Sox ace Pedro Martinez was pitching. Sox analysts had demonstrated conclusively that Martinez became much easier for opposing batters to hit after about 7 innings or 105 pitches (that year, the opposing team's batting average against Martinez for pitches 91–105 was .231; for pitches 106–120 it was .370). They had warned manager Grady Little that by no means should Martinez be left in the game after that point. Yet when Martinez predictably began to falter late in the seventh, Little let him keep pitching into the eighth (even against the advice of his pitching coach), and the Yankees shelled Martinez. The

Yanks won the ALCS, but Little lost his job. It's a powerful story of what can happen if frontline managers and employees don't go along with the analytical program. Fortunately for long-suffering Red Sox fans (including one of the authors of this volume), the combination of numbers and money proved insurmountable in the 2004 season, and the Sox broke the eighty-six-year World Series championship drought.

Analytical competition has not fully triumphed in baseball, however. Some teams—including some perennially good teams, such as the Atlanta Braves—still rely heavily on traditional scouting criteria, although they use numbers too. The Braves' general manager, John Schuerholz, argued in an interview that "to suggest that new, statistical, chrome-plated, digitally enhanced, new-age-thinking statistics alone can replace scouting instincts and human judgment and analysis, I take great exception to that. So what we do is use both."[15] St. Louis Cardinals coach Tony La Russa (whose team won the 2006 World Series), one of the best coaches in the game, brilliantly combines analytics with intuition to decide when to substitute a charged-up player in the batting lineup or whether to hire a spark plug personality to improve morale. In his recent book, *Three Nights in August*, Buzz Bissinger describes that balance: "La Russa appreciated the information generated by computers. He studied the rows and the columns. But he also knew they could take you only so far in baseball, maybe even confuse you with a fog of overanalysis. As far as he knew, there was no way to quantify desire. And those numbers told him exactly what he needed to know when added to twenty-four years of managing experience."[16]

Analytics have also spread to professional football. The New England Patriots, for example, have been particularly successful of late, winning three Super Bowls in four years. The team uses data and analytical models extensively, both on and off the field. In-depth analytics help the team select its players and stay below the salary cap (last year the team had the twenty-fourth-highest payroll in the National Football League). The team selects players without using the scouting services that other teams employ, and it rates potential draft choices on such nontraditional factors as intelligence and willingness to subsume personal ego for the benefit of the team.

The Patriots also make extensive use of analytics for on-the-field decisions. They employ statistics, for example, to decide whether to punt or "go for it" on fourth down, whether to try for one point or two after a touchdown, and whether to challenge a referee's ruling. Both its coaches

and players are renowned for their extensive study of game films and statistics, and head coach Bill Belichick has been known to peruse articles
by academic economists on statistical probabilities of football outcomes.
Off the field, the team uses detailed analytics to assess and improve the
"total fan experience." At every home game, for example, twenty to
twenty-five people have specific assignments to make quantitative measurements of the stadium food, parking, personnel, bathroom cleanli-
ness, and other factors. External vendors of services are monitored for
contract renewal and have incentives to improve their performance.[17]

Other NFL teams that make extensive usage of statistics include the
Kansas City Chiefs, Tennessee Titans, and Green Bay Packers. The Titans, for example, have determined that the traditional performance
measures of yards allowed or gained are relatively meaningless, and
have come up with alternative measures. The Packers analyzed game
films of one running back with a fumbling problem, and determined
that the fumbles only happened when the player's elbow wasn't hori-
zontal to the ground when he was hit.[18] Despite the success of the Patriots and these other teams, many teams in the NFL have yet to grasp the
nature and value of analytical competition.

Professional basketball has historically been less quantitatively oriented than baseball or football, but the numeric approach is beginning
to take off there as well. Several teams, including the high-performing
San Antonio Spurs, have hired statistical consultants or statistically oriented executives. The Houston Rockets have recently selected as general manager a young, quantitatively oriented executive who previously
managed information systems and analytics for the Boston Celtics.
Daryl Morey, an MIT MBA, considers baseball sabermetrician Bill
James to be his role model, and argues that analytics in basketball are
similar to those for moneyball in baseball. "It's the same principle.
Generate wins for fewer dollars."[19] As in baseball and football, teams
and their analysts are pursuing new measures, such as a player's value
to the team when on the court versus when off of it (called the Roland
Rating after amateur statistician Roland Beech).

Analytical competition is taking root not only in U.S. sports. Some
soccer teams in Europe have also begun to employ similar techniques.
AC Milan, one of the leading teams in Europe, uses predictive models to
prevent player injuries by analyzing physiological, orthopedic, and psy-
chological data from a variety of sources. Its Milan Lab identifies the risk
factors that are most likely to be associated with an injury for each player.

The lab also assesses potential players to add to the team. Several members of the World Cup–winning Italy national team trained at Milan Lab. The Bolton Wanderers, a fast-rising English soccer team, are known for the manager's use of extensive data to evaluate player performance and team strategies. The team also uses analytics to identify its most valuable customers and to offer them benefits that help build loyalty.

Why all this activity in professional sports, and what difference does it make for other types of organizations? There are many themes that could cut across sports and business. Perhaps the most important lesson from professional sports analytics is its focus on the human resource—on choosing and keeping the best players at the lowest price. This is not a widespread practice in the business "talent management" domain, but perhaps it should be. As executive and individual contributor salaries continue to rise, it may be time to begin to analyze and gather data on which people perform well under what circumstances, and to ensure that the right players are on the team. A few firms are beginning to adopt a more analytical approach to human resource management, but sports teams are still far ahead of other organizations.

Analytical competition in sports also illustrates the point that analysis rises first when sufficient data is present to analyze. If there is a business area in which large amounts of data are available for the first time, it will probably soon become a playing field for analytical competition. Analytical innovators in professional sports also often create new measures, and businesspeople should do the same.

While analytics is a somewhat abstract and complex subject, its adoption in professional sports illustrates the human nature of the process. When a team embraces analytical competition, it's because a leader makes a decision to do so. That decision can often be traced to the leader's own background and experiences. Analytical competition—whether in sports or business—is almost always a story involving people and leadership.

It's also no accident that the sports teams that have embraced analytical competition have generally done well. They won't win championships every year, of course, but analytical competitors have been successful in every sport in which they have arisen. However, as analytical competition spreads—and it spreads quickly—teams will have to continue innovating and building their analytical capabilities if they wish to stay in front. Whatever the approach to competition, no team (or firm) can afford to rest on its laurels.

What's in This Book

We've attempted to lay out the general outlines of analytical competition in this chapter and to provide a few examples in the worlds of business and sports. There are many more examples to come, and throughout part I of the book, we'll go into much more detail about what it means to compete on analytics and how companies can move in that direction. Chapter 2 describes the specific attributes of firms that compete on analytics and lays out a five-stage model of just how analytically oriented an organization is. Chapter 3 describes how analytics contribute to better business performance, and includes some data and analysis on that topic. Chapters 4 and 5 describe a number of applications of analytics in business; they are grouped into internally oriented applications and those primarily involving external relationships with customers and suppliers.

In part II of the book, our goal is to discuss the key steps and capabilities involved in analytical competition. We begin that part with a discussion in chapter 6 of the overall road map for analytical competition. Chapter 7 is about the most important factor in making a company analytical: its people. Chapter 8 is about the important resources of technology and data, and how they can be combined in an overall analytical architecture. We conclude the book in chapter 9 with a discussion of the future directions that analytical competition might take.

We do our best to help organizations embark upon this path to business and organizational success. However, it's important to remember that this is just an overview. There are many books on how to implement business intelligence, how to create and modify analytical models in such areas as supply chain and marketing, and how to do basic quantitative and statistical analysis. Our goal is not to give businesspeople all the knowledge they'll ever need to do serious analytical work, but rather to get you excited about the possibilities for analytical competition and motivated enough to pursue further study.

2

WHAT MAKES AN ANALYTICAL
COMPETITOR?

Defining the Common
Key Attributes of Such Companies

WHAT DOES IT MEAN TO compete on analytics? We define an *analytical competitor* as an organization that uses analytics extensively and systematically to outthink and outexecute the competition. In this chapter, we'll describe the key attributes of companies that compete on analytics, and describe the levels and stages of these attributes that we found in researching actual organizations.

Among the firms we studied, we found that the most analytically sophisticated and successful had four common key characteristics: (1) analytics supported a strategic, distinctive capability; (2) the approach to and management of analytics was enterprise-wide; (3) senior management was committed to the use of analytics; and (4) the company made a significant strategic bet on analytics-based competition. We found each of these attributes present in the companies that were most aggressively pursuing analytical approaches to business.

We don't know, of course, exactly how many analytical competitors there are, but we do have data allowing a good estimate. In a global survey of 371 medium to large firms conducted in late 2005, we asked respondents (IT executives or business executives familiar with their companies' enterprise IT applications) how much analytical capability their organizations had. The highest category was described by the statement "Analytical capability is a key element of strategy" for the business. Ten percent of the respondents selected that category. According to our detailed analysis of the data, perhaps half of these firms are full-bore analytical competitors. There may be slightly more or fewer, but we don't know of any better estimate.

Primary Attributes of Analytical Competitors

Next, we'll describe how several of the companies we studied exemplify the four attributes of analytical competition. True analytical competitors exhibit all four; less advanced organizations may have only one or two at best.

Support of a Strategic, Distinctive Capability

It stands to reason that if analytics are to support competitive strategy, they must be in support of an important and distinctive capability. As we mentioned in the first chapter, the capability varies by organization and industry, and might involve supply chains, pricing and revenue management, customer service, customer loyalty, or human resource management. At Netflix, of course, the primary focus for analytics is on predicting customer movie preferences. At Harrah's, it's on customer loyalty and service. Marriott International's primary analytical orientation is on revenue management. Wal-Mart obviously emphasizes supply chain analytics. Professional sports teams generally focus on human resources, or choosing the right players.

Having a distinctive capability means that the organization views this aspect of its business as what sets it apart from competitors and as what makes it successful in the marketplace. In companies without this strategic focus, analytical capabilities are just a utility to be applied to a variety of business problems without regard for their significance.

Of course, not all businesses have a distinctive capability. They usually suffer when they don't. It's not obvious, for example, what Kmart's, US Airways', or General Motors' distinctive capabilities are. To the outside observer, they don't do anything substantially better than their competitors—and their customers and potential shareholders have noticed. Without a distinctive capability, you can't be an analytical competitor, because there is no clear process or activity for analytics to support.

It's also possible that the distinctive capability an organization chooses would not be well supported by analytics—at least this has been true in the past. If the strategic decisions an organization makes are intuitive or experience based and cannot be made analytically, it wouldn't make sense to try to compete on statistics and fact-based decisions. We mentioned the fashion and executive search businesses in this regard in chapter 1. One might add management consulting to this list, in that most consulting advice is based on experience rather than analytics. We suspect, however, that in each of these industries there is the potential for analytical competition and that some firm will adopt it at some point in time. Fashion businesses could try to decompose and predict the elements of consumer taste. Executive search firms could build their businesses around a database of what kinds of executives perform well under certain circumstances. And consultants (and lawyers and investment bankers, for that matter) could base their advice to clients on detailed statistical analysis of what management approaches have been effective in specified business situations. They could perhaps transform their industries by taking an analytical approach to strategy.

A corollary of this factor is that analytical competitors pay careful attention to measures of the distinctive capabilities in their businesses. They engage in both *exploitation* and *exploration* of measures—they exploit existing measures to a considerable degree and are early to explore new measures. We've already discussed professional baseball, where teams like Oakland's have moved to new measures of player performance. Consumer finance is another industry with a strong emphasis on developing new metrics.

Because there are many quantitative transactions in consumer financial services, it's relatively easy to employ measures in decision making. Perhaps the most commonly used measure in consumer finance is the credit or FICO score, which is an indicator of the customer's creditworthiness. There are many possible credit scores, but only one official FICO score. (FICO scores are based on an algorithm developed by Fair, Isaac and Company [currently Fair Isaac Corporation] in 1989. Now, the three major credit bureaus have created a competitor, the Vantage Score, that, unlike the FICO score, is consistent with all credit ratings; in Europe, some financial services firms employ credit scores from Scorex.) Virtually every consumer finance firm in the United States uses the FICO score to make consumer credit decisions and to decide what interest rate to charge. Analytical banking competitors such as Capital One, however, adopted it earlier and more aggressively than other firms. Their distinctive capability was finding out which customers were most desirable in terms of paying considerable interest without defaulting on their loans. After FICO scores had become pervasive in banking, they began to spread to the insurance industry. Again, highly analytical firms such as Progressive determined that consumers with high FICO scores not only were more likely to pay back loans, but also were less likely to have automobile accidents. Therefore, they began to charge lower premiums for customers with higher FICO scores.

Today, however, there is little distinction in simply using a FICO score in banking or property and casualty insurance. The new frontiers are in applying credit scores in other industries and in mining data about them to refine decision making. Some analysts are predicting, for example, that credit scores will soon be applied in making life and health insurance decisions and pricing of premiums. At least one health insurance company is exploring whether the use of credit scores might make it possible to avoid requiring an expensive physical examination before issuing a health policy. One professor also notes that they might be used for employment screening:

> It is uncommon to counsel individuals with financial problems who don't have other kinds of problems. You're more likely to miss days at work, be less productive on the job, as well as have marriage and other relationship problems if you are struggling financially. It makes sense that if you have a low credit score that you are more likely to have problems in other areas of life. Employers looking to screen a large number of applicants could easily see a credit score as an effective way to narrow the field.[1]

Since credit scores are pervasive, some firms are beginning to try to disaggregate credit scores and determine which factors are most closely associated with the desired outcome. Progressive Insurance and Capital One, for example, are both reputed to be disaggregating and analyzing credit scores to determine which customers with relatively low scores might be better risks than their overall scores would predict.

One last point on the issue of distinctive capabilities. These mission-critical capabilities should be the organization's primary analytical target. Yet we've noticed that over time, analytical competitors tend to move into a variety of analytical domains. Marriott started its analytical work in the critical area of revenue management but later moved into loyalty program analysis and Web metrics analysis. At Netflix, the most strategic application may be predicting customer movie preferences, but the company also employs testing and detailed analysis in its supply chain and its advertising. Harrah's started in loyalty and service but also does detailed analyses of its slot machine pricing and placement, the design of its Web site, and many other issues in its business. Wal-Mart, Progressive Insurance, and the hospital supply distributor Owens & Minor are all examples of firms that started with an internal analytical focus but have broadened it externally—to suppliers in the case of Wal-Mart and to customers for the other two firms. Analytical competitors need a primary focus for their analytical activity, but once an analytical, test-and-learn culture has been created, it's impossible to stop it from spreading.

An Enterprise-Level Approach to and Management of Analytics

Companies and organizations that compete analytically don't entrust analytical activities just to one group within the company or to a collection of disparate employees across the organization. They manage analytics as an organization or enterprise and ensure that no process or business unit is optimized at the expense of another unless it is strategically important to do so. At Harrah's, for example, when Gary Loveman began the company's move into analytical competition, he had all the company's casino property heads report to him, and ensured that they implemented the company's marketing and customer service programs in the same way. Before this, each property had been a "fiefdom," managed by "feudal lords with occasional interruptions from the king or queen who passed through town."[2] This made it virtually impossible for Harrah's to implement marketing and loyalty initiatives encouraging cross-market play.

Enterprise-level management also means ensuring that the data and analyses are made available broadly throughout the organization and that the proper care is taken to manage data and analyses efficiently and effectively. If decisions that drive the company's success are made on overly narrow data, incorrect data, or faulty analysis, the consequences could be severe. Therefore, analytical competitors make the management of analytics and the data on which they are based an organization-wide activity. For example, one of the reasons that RBC Financial Group (the best-known unit of which is Royal Bank of Canada) has been a successful analytical competitor is that it decided early on (in the 1970s) that all customer data would be owned by the enterprise and held in a central customer information file. Bank of America attributes its analytical capabilities around asset and interest-rate risk exposure to the fact that risk was managed in a consistent way across the enterprise. Many other banks have been limited in their ability to assess the overall profitability or loyalty of customers because different divisions or product groups have different and incompatible ways to define and record customer data.

An enterprise approach is a departure from the past for many organizations. Analytics have largely been either an individual or a departmental activity in the past and largely remain so today in companies that don't compete on analytics. For example, in a 2005 survey of 220 organizations' approaches to the management of business intelligence (which, remember, also includes some nonanalytical activities, such as reporting), only 45 percent said that their use of business intelligence was either "organizational" or "global," with 53 percent responding "in my department," "departmental," "regional," or "individual." In the same survey, only 22 percent of firms reported a formal needs assessment process across the enterprise; 29 percent did no needs assessment at all; and 43 percent assessed business intelligence needs at the divisional or departmental level.[3] The reasons for this decentralization are easy to understand. A particular quantitatively focused department, such as quality, marketing, or pricing, may have used analytics in going about its work, without affecting the overall strategy or management approach of the enterprise. Perhaps its activities should have been elevated into a strategic resource, with broader access and greater management attention. Most frequently, however, these departmental analytical applications remained in the background.

Another possibility is that analytics might have been left entirely up to individuals within those departments. In such cases, analytics took place primarily on individual spreadsheets. While it's great for individual employees to use data and analysis to support their decisions, individually created and managed spreadsheets are not the best way to manage analytics for an enterprise. For one thing, they can contain errors. Research by one academic suggests that between 20 percent and 40 percent of user-created spreadsheets contain errors; the more spreadsheets, the more errors.[4] While there are no estimates of the frequency of errors for enterprise-level analytics, they could at least involve

WHAT MAKES AN ANALYTICAL COMPETITOR? • 29

processes to control and eliminate errors that would be difficult to impose at the individual level.

A second problem with individual analytics is that they create "multiple versions of the truth," while most organizations seek only one. If, for example, there are multiple databases and calculations of the lifetime value of a company's customers across different individuals and departments, it will be difficult to focus the entire organization's attention on its best customers. If there are different versions of financial analytics across an organization, the consequences could be dire indeed—for example, extending to jail for senior executives under Sarbanes-Oxley legislation. Hence there are considerable advantages to managing key data and analytics at the enterprise level, so that there is only one version of critical business information and analytical results for decision making. Then, of course, the information and results can be distributed widely for use across the organization. Harrah's, for example, calls its management approach for customer analytics "centrally driven, broadly distributed."

Enterprise management may take a variety of forms. For some organizations, it may mean only that central IT groups manage the data and procure and install the needed business intelligence software. For others, it may mean that a central analytical services group assists executives with analysis and decision making. As we'll discuss in chapter 7, a number of firms have established such groups.

From an IT standpoint, another approach to enterprise-level management of analytics is the establishment of a *business intelligence competency center*, or BICC. According to SAS, a BICC is defined as "a cross-functional team with a permanent, formal organizational structure. It is owned and staffed by the [company] and has defined tasks, roles, responsibilities and processes for supporting and promoting the effective use of business intelligence across the organization."[5]

In the business intelligence survey of 220 firms described earlier, 23 percent of respondents said their firm already had a BICC. The purpose of such groups is often limited to IT-related issues. However, it could easily be extended to include development and refinement of analytical approaches and tools. For example, at Schneider National, a large trucking and logistics company, the central analytical group (called engineering and research) is a part of the chief information officer organization, and addresses BICC-type functions as well as working with internal and external customers on analytical applications and problems.

Senior Management Commitment

The adoption of a broad analytical approach to business requires changes in culture, process, behavior, and skills for multiple employees. Such changes don't happen by accident; they must be led by senior executives with a passion for analytics and fact-based decision making. Ideally, the primary advocate should be the CEO, and indeed we found several chief executives who were driving the shift to analytics at their firms. These included Gary Loveman, CEO of Harrah's; Jeff Bezos, the founder and CEO of Amazon.com; Rich Fairbank, the founder and CEO of Capital One; Reed Hastings of Netflix; and Barry Beracha, formerly CEO of Sara Lee Bakery Group. Each of these executives has stated both internally and publicly that their companies are engaged in some form of analytical competition. For example, Fairbank commented, "It's all about collecting information on 200 million people you'd never meet, and on the basis of that information, making a series of very critical long-term decisions about lending them money and hoping they would pay you back."[6]

Fairbank summarizes this approach as "information-based strategy." Beracha, before he retired as CEO of Sara Lee Bakery, simply kept a sign on his desk reading, "In God we trust; all others bring data" (a quote originally attributed to W. Edwards Deming). Loveman frequently asks employees, "Do we think, or do we know?" Anyone presenting ideas for initiatives or strategies is pressed for supporting evidence. Loveman has hired into Harrah's a number of very analytical senior and middle managers. He also listed three reasons why employees could be fired from Harrah's: ". . . you don't harass women, you don't steal, and you've got to have a control group."[7]

Loveman provides an excellent example of how a CEO—and ideally an entire executive team—who constantly pushes employees to use testing and analysis, and make fact-based decisions, can change an organization's culture. He's not just supportive of analytics—he's passionate on the subject.

Without the push from the top, it's rare to find a firm making the cultural changes necessary to become an analytical competitor. We know it's a bit of a cliché to say that an idea needs the passionate support of the CEO or other senior general managers, but in our research on analytical competitors, we simply didn't find any without such committed and broad support from the executive suite. We found some firms, for example, in which single functional or business unit leaders (such as heads of marketing or research) were trying to engineer an analytically oriented shift in their firms but weren't able to sufficiently change the culture by themselves. This doesn't mean, of course, that such an executive couldn't lead a change like this under other circumstances, and we did find organizations in which lower-level advocates were making progress on changing the culture. Any cross-functional or cross-department change, and certainly any enterprise-wide effort, clearly requires the support and attention of executives senior enough to direct and coordinate efforts in those separate units.

How does an executive develop a passion for analytics? It helps, of course, if they learn it in school. We've mentioned the math teacher background of Reed Hastings at Netflix. Loveman of Harrah's has a PhD in economics from MIT and taught at Harvard Business School. Bezos from Amazon.com was a quantitatively oriented A+ engineering and computer science student at Princeton. Fairbanks and New England Patriots COO Jonathan Kraft were MBAs and analytically oriented management consultants before taking their jobs at their respective analytical competitors. Chris Lofgren, the president and CEO of Schneider National, has a PhD in operations research. It's obviously a desirable situation when a CEO can go toe-to-toe with the "propeller heads" in the analytical department.

However, not every analytical executive has or needs such an extensive background. Statistics and data analysis are taught at virtually every college in the land. And a CEO doesn't have to be smarter or more quantitatively oriented than all of his or her employees. What is necessary is a willingness to delve into analytical approaches, the ability to engage in discussions with quantitative experts, and the fortitude to push others to think and act analytically.

There are several corollaries of the senior management commitment factor. CEO orientation drives not only the culture and mind share directed to analytics but also the level and persistence of the investment in people, IT, data, and so forth. It is no simple matter, as we will describe in subsequent chapters, to assemble these resources, and it can require substantial time.

Barclays's consumer finance organization, for example, had a "five-year plan" to build the unit's capabilities for analytical competition.[8] Executives in the consumer business had seen the powerful analytical transformations wrought by such U.S. banks as Capital One, and felt that Barclays was underleveraging its very large customer base in the United Kingdom. In adopting an analytical strategy, the company had to adjust virtually all aspects of its consumer business, including the interest rates it charges, the way it underwrites risk and sets credit limits, how it services accounts, its approach to controlling fraud, and how it cross-sells other products. It had to make its data on 13 million Barclay-Card customers integrated and of sufficient quality to support detailed analyses. It had to undertake a large number of small tests to begin learning how to attract and retain the best customers at the lowest price. New people with quantitative analysis skills had to be hired, and new systems had to be built. Given all these activities, it's no surprise that it took from 1998 to 2003 to put the information-based customer strategy in place. A single senior executive, Keith Coulter (now managing director for Barclays U.K. consumer cards and loans), oversaw these changes during the period. Coulter couldn't have worked out and executed on such a long-term plan without clear evidence of commitment from Barclays's most senior executives.

Large-Scale Ambition

A final way to define analytical competitors is by the results they aspire to achieve. The analytical competitors we studied had bet their future success on analytics-based strategies. In retrospect, the strategies appear very logical and rational. At the time, however, they were radical departures from standard industry practice. The founders of Capital One, for example, shopped their idea for "information-based strategy" to all the leaders of the credit card industry and found no takers. When Signet Bank accepted their terms and rebuilt its strategy and processes for credit cards around the new ideas, it was a huge gamble. The company was betting its future, at least in that business unit, on the analytical approach.

Not all attempts to create analytical competition will be successful, of course. But the scale and scope of results from such efforts should at least be large enough to affect organizational fortunes. Incremental, tactical uses of analytics will yield minor results; strategic, competitive uses should yield major ones.

There are many ways to measure the results of analytical activity, but the most obvious is with money. A single analytical initiative should result in savings or revenue increases in the hundreds of millions or billions for a large organization. There are many possible examples. One of the earliest was the idea of "yield management" at American Airlines, which greatly improved the company's fortunes in the 1980s. This technique, which involves optimizing the price at which each airline seat is sold to a passenger, is credited with bringing in $1.2 billion for American over three years and with putting some feisty competitors (such as People Express) out of business.[9] At Deere & Company, a new way of optimizing inventory (called "direct derivative estimation of nonstationary inventory") saved the company $1.2 billion in inventory costs between 2000 and 2005.[10] Procter & Gamble used operations research methods to reorganize sourcing and distribution approaches in the mid-1990s and saved the company $200 million in costs.[11]

The results of analytical competition can also be measured in overall revenues and profits, market share, and customer loyalty. If a company can't see any impact on such critical measures of its nonfinancial and financial performance, it's not really competing on analytics. At Harrah's, for example, the company increased its market share from 36 percent to 43 percent between 1998 (when it started its customer loyalty analytics initiative) and 2004.[12] Over that same time period, the company experienced "same store" sales gains in twenty-three of twenty-four quarters, and play by customers across multiple markets increased every year. Before the adoption of these approaches, the company had failed to meet revenue and profit expectations for seven straight years. Capital One, which became a public company in 1994, increased earnings per share and return on equity by at least 20 percent each year over its first decade. Barclays's information-based customer management strategy in its U.K. consumer finance business led to lower recruitment costs for customers, higher customer balances with lower risk exposure, and a 25 percent increase in revenue per customer account—all over the first three years of the program. As we'll discuss in chapter 3, the analytical competitors we've studied tend to be relatively high performers.

These four factors, we feel, are roughly equivalent in defining analytical competition. Obviously, they are not entirely independent of each other. If senior executive leadership is committed and has built the strategy around an analytics-led distinctive capability, it's likely that the organization will adopt an enterprise-wide approach and that the results sought from analytics will reflect the strategic orientation. Therefore, we view them as four pillars supporting an analytical platform (see figure 2-1). If any one fell, the others would have difficulty compensating.

FIGURE 2-1

Four pillars of analytical competition

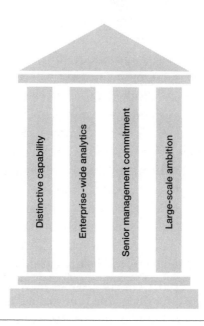

Of all the four, however, senior executive commitment is perhaps the most important because it can make the others possible. It's no accident that many of the organizations we describe became analytical competitors when a new CEO arrived (e.g., Loveman at Harrah's) or when they were founded by CEOs with a strong analytical orientation from the beginning (Hastings at Netflix or Bezos at Amazon.com). Sometimes the change comes from a new generation of managers in a family business. At the winemaker E. & J. Gallo, when Joe Gallo, the son of one of the firm's founding brothers, became CEO, he focused much more than the previous generation of leaders on data and analysis—first in sales and later in other functions, including the assessment of customer taste. At the New England Patriots National Football League team, the involvement in the team by Jonathan Kraft, the son of owner Bob Kraft and a former management consultant, helped move the team in a more analytical direction in terms of both on-field issues like play selection and team composition and off-field issues affecting the fan experience.

Assessing the Degree of Analytical Competition

If these four factors are the hallmarks or defining factors of analytical competition, we can begin to assess organizations by how much or how little they have of them. To do so, we have identified five stages of analytical competition, as seen in figure 2-2. The key attributes for each stage are listed in table 2-1. Like the well-known "capability maturity model" for software development, these stages can describe the path that an organization can follow from having virtually no analytical capabilities to being a serious analytical competitor. In chapter 6, we describe the overall road map for moving through these stages.

Stage 5 organizations are full-blown *analytical competitors*, with high degrees of each of the four factors described earlier. Their analytical activities are clearly in support of a distinctive capability, they are taking an enterprise-wide approach, their executives are passionate and driving, and their analytical initiatives are aimed at substantial results. Some of the firms that fall into this category include Google, Harrah's, Amazon.com, Capital One, Progressive, Netflix, Wal-Mart, and Yahoo!, as well as several sports teams we've discussed. These organizations could

FIGURE 2-2

The five stages of analytical competition

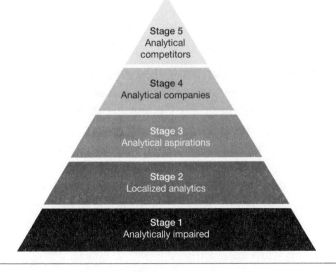

TABLE 2-1

Competing on analytics stages model

Stage	Distinctive capability/level of insights	Questions asked	Objective	Metrics/measure/value
1 Analytically impaired	Negligible, "flying blind"	What happened in our business?	Get accurate data to improve operations	None
2 Localized analytics	Local and opportunistic— may not be supporting company's distinctive capabilities	What can we do to improve this activity? How can we understand our business better?	Use analytics to improve one or more functional activities	ROI of individual applications
3 Analytical aspirations	Begin efforts for more integrated data and analytics	What's happening now? Can we extrapolate existing trends?	Use analytics to improve a distinctive capability	Future performance and market value
4 Analytical companies	Enterprise-wide perspective, able to use analytics for point advantage, know what to do to get to next level, but not quite there	How can we use analytics to innovate and differentiate?	Build broad analytic capability— analytics for differentiation	Analytics are an important driver of performance and value
5 Analytical competitors	Enterprise-wide, big results, sustainable advantage	What's next? What's possible? How do we stay ahead?	Analytical master—fully competing on analytics	Analytics are the primary driver of performance and value

always apply their analytical capabilities even more broadly—and they are constantly doing so—but they already have them focused on the most significant capability their strategy requires. In our sample of thirty-two firms that are at least somewhat oriented to analytics, eleven were stage 5 analytical competitors. However, we sought out firms that fit in this category, so by no means should this be taken as an indicator of their overall prevalence. From our other research, we'd estimate that no more than 5 percent of large firms would be in this category overall (i.e., half of the percentage in our survey saying that "analytical capability is a key element of strategy"; the other half would be stage 4). Most of the stage 5 organizations we discovered, as might be predicted, were information-intensive services firms, with four firms in financial services. Several were also dot-com firms. However, it's difficult to generalize about industries for analytical competition, since we found stage 5 organizations in several industry categories.

Stage 4 organizations, our *analytical companies,* are on the verge of analytical competition but still face a few minor hurdles to get there in full measure. For example, they have the skill but lack the out-and-out will to compete on this basis. Perhaps the CEO and executive team are supportive of an analytical focus but are not passionate about competing on this basis. Or perhaps there is substantial analytical activity, but it is not targeted at a distinctive capability. With only a small increase in emphasis, the companies could move into analytical competitor status. We found seven organizations in this category.

For example, one stage 4 consumer products firm we studied had strong analytical activities in several areas of the business. However, it wasn't clear that analytics were closely bound to the organization's strategy, and neither analytics nor the likely synonyms for them were mentioned in the company's recent annual reports. Analytics or information was not mentioned as one of the firm's strategic competencies. Granted, there are people within this company—and all of the stage 4 companies we studied—who are working diligently to make the company an analytical competitor, but they aren't yet influential enough to make it happen.

The organizations at stage 3 do grasp the value and the promise of analytical competition, but they face major capability hurdles and are a long way from overcoming them. Because of the importance of executive awareness and commitment, we believe that just having that is enough to put the organization at a higher stage and on the full-steam-ahead path that we described in the first chapter. We found seven organizations in this position. Some have only recently articulated the vision and have not really begun implementing it. Others have very high levels of functional or business unit autonomy and are having difficulty mounting a cohesive approach to analytics across the enterprise.

One multiline insurance company, for example, had a CEO with the vision of using data, analytics, and a strong customer orientation in the fashion of the stage 5 firm Progressive, an auto insurance company with a history of technological and analytical innovation. But the multiline company had only recently begun to expand its analytical orientation beyond the traditionally quantitative actuarial function, and thus far there was little cooperation across the life and property and casualty business units.

We also interviewed executives from three different pharmaceutical firms, and we categorized two of the three into stage 3 at present. It was clear to all the managers that analytics were the key to the future of the industry. The combination of clinical, genomic, and proteomic data will lead to an analytical transformation and an environment of personalized medicine. Yet both the science and the application of informatics in these domains are as yet incomplete.[13] Each of our interviewees admitted that their company, and the rest of the industry, has a long way to go before mastering their analytical future. One of the companies, Vertex Pharmaceuticals, has made significant progress toward analytical competition—not by striving toward the analytical holy grail described earlier, but by making more analytical decisions in virtually every phase of drug development and marketing.

Despite the implementation issues faced by stage 3 firms, because executive demand is one of the most important aspects of a company's analytical orientation—and because sufficient interest from executives can drive a great deal of change relatively quickly—we'd put these firms ahead of those that may even have more analytical activity but less interest from executives. We refer to them as having *competitive aspirations* with regard to analytics.

Stage 2 organizations exhibit the typical *localized analytics* approach to "business intelligence" in the past—that is, an emphasis on reporting with pockets of analytical activity—but they don't measure up to the standard of competing on analytics. They do analytical work, but they have no intention of competing on it. We found six of these firms in our study, although they would be much more common in a random sample, and perhaps the largest group.

By no means have analytics transformed the way these organizations do business. Marketing, for example, may be identifying optimal customers or modeling demand, but the company still markets to all customers and creates supply independent of the demand models. Their business intelligence activities produce economic benefits but not enough to affect the company's competitive strategy. What they primarily lack is any vision of analytical competition from senior executives. Several of the firms have some of the same technology as firms at higher stages of analytical activity, but they have not put it to strategic use.

Stage 1 organizations have some desire to become more analytical, but thus far they lack both the will and the skill to do so. We call them *analytically impaired* organizations. They face some substantial barriers—both human and technical—to analytical competition and are still focused on putting basic, integrated transaction functionality and high-quality data in place. They may also lack the hardware, software, and skills to do substantial analysis. They certainly lack any interest in analytical competition on the part of senior executives. To the degree that they have any analytical activity at all, it is both small and local. At a state government organization we researched, for example, the following barriers were cited in our interview notes from April 4, 2005:

> [Manager interviewed] noted that there is not as great a sense in government that "time is money" and therefore that something needs to happen. Moreover, decision making is driven more by the budget and less by strategy. What this means is that decisions are as a rule very short-term focused on the current fiscal year and not characterized by a longer-term perspective. Finally, [interviewee] noted that one of the other impediments to developing a fact-based culture is that the technical tools today are not really adequate. Despite these difficulties, there is a great deal of interest on the part of the governor and the head of administration and finance to bring a new reform perspective to decision making and more of an analytical perspective. They are also starting to recruit staff with more of these analytical skills.

As a result of these deficiencies, stage 1 organizations are not yet even on the path to becoming analytical competitors, even though they have a desire to be. Because we only selected organizations to interview that wanted to compete on analytics, we included only two stage 1 organizations—a state government and an engineering firm (and even that firm is becoming somewhat more analytical about its human resources). However, such organizations, and those at stage 2, probably constitute the majority of all organizations in the world at large. Many firms today don't have a single definition of the customer, for example, and hence they can't use customer data across the organization to segment and select the best customers. They can't connect demand and supply information, so they can't optimize their supply chains. They can't understand the relationship between their nonfinancial performance indicators and their financial results. They may not even have a

single definitive list of their employees—much less the ability to analyze employee traits. Such basic data issues are all too common among
most firms today.

We have referred to these different categories as *stages* rather than
levels because most organizations need to go through each one. However, with sufficiently motivated senior executives, it may be possible to
skip a stage or at least move rapidly though them. We haven't yet observed the progress of analytical orientation within a set of firms over
time. But we would bet that an organization that was in a hurry to get to
stage 5 could hire the people, buy the technology, and pound data into
shape within a year or two. The greatest constraint on rapid movement
through the stages would be changing the basic business processes and
behaviors of the organization and its people. That's always the most difficult and time-consuming part of any major organizational change.

In the next chapter, we describe the relationship between analytical
activity and business performance. We discuss analytical applications
for key processes in two subsequent chapters. The first, chapter 4, describes the role that analytics play in internally oriented processes, such
as finance and human resource management. Chapter 5 focuses on
using analytics to enhance organizations' externally oriented activities,
including customer and supplier specific interactions. Before we get
there, we will explore the link between organizations that have high analytical orientations and high-performance businesses.

3

ANALYTICS AND BUSINESS PERFORMANCE

Transforming the Ability to Compete on Analytics
into a Lasting Competitive Advantage

IN THE 1980S, TWO FINANCIAL services consultants, Richard Fairbank and Nigel Morris, identified a major problem in the credit card industry, as well as a potential solution. The problem was that the industry lacked a focus on the individual customer, and the solution came in the form of technology-driven analytics.

Fairbank and Morris believed that insights from data analysis would enable a company to discover, target, and serve the most profitable credit customers while leaving other firms with less profitable customers. They pitched this idea, their "information-based market strategy," to more than fifteen national retail banks before Virginia-based Signet Bank hired them to work in its bank card division. Signet was hardly a leading competitor in credit cards at the time.

Over the next two years, the duo ran thousands of analytical tests on Signet's customer database—much to the chagrin of the company's previous, and largely intuitive, experts. They discovered that the most profitable customers were people who borrowed large amounts quickly and then paid off the balances slowly. At the time, the credit card industry treated such customers just as they treated people who made small purchases and paid their balances off in full every month. Recognizing an opportunity, the team created the industry's first balance-transfer card. As the first card that targeted debtors as valued, not just valuable, customers, it quickly took off within the industry. Ultimately, Fairbank and Morris's success with analytics led Signet to spin off its bank card division as a company called Capital One.

Today, Capital One runs about three hundred experiments per business day, on average, to improve its ability to target individual customers. These tests provide a relatively low-cost way for the company to judge how successful products and programs would be before it engages in full-scale marketing. In its savings business, for example, Capital One found that its experiments in terms of CD interest rates, rollover incentives, minimum balances, and so forth had very predictable effects on retention rates and new money coming into the bank. Through such analyses, the savings business increased retention by 87 percent and lowered the cost of acquiring a new account by 83 percent.

Through this analytical approach to marketing, Capital One is able to identify and serve new market segments before its peers can. The key to this ability is the company's closed loop of testing, learning, and acting on new opportunities. The firm's knowledge of what works and what doesn't forms the basis of a strategic asset that enables it to avoid approaches and customers that won't pay off. Few companies are truly set up to apply the principles of this test-and-learn approach, but Capital One's entire distinctive capability is built on it.

Capital One's analytical prowess has transformed the organization into a *Fortune* 200 company with an enviable record of growth and profitability. The value of its stock has increased by 1,000 percent over the past ten years, outpacing the S&P 500 index by a factor of 10. By comparison with its largest competitors, Capital One's stock has increased two to four times faster over the same period. Analytics are at the heart of the company's ability to consistently outperform its peers and sustain its competitive advantage.

Now consider a long-established company that has also become an analytical competitor: Marriott International, the global hotel and resort firm. Marriott's focus on fact-based decision making and analytics is deeply embedded in the corporate culture and lore. As one senior executive put it, "Everything is based on metrics here." This orientation was instilled as early as the 1950s, when founder J. Willard Marriott used to observe the occupancy of cars pulling into his motel's parking lot in order to charge the rate for a double room, if appropriate.

Over the last twenty years, Marriott has built on J. W. Marriott's early labor-intensive foray into *revenue management*—the process by which hotels establish the optimal price for their rooms (the industry's "inventory"). The economics are simple: if a hotel can predict the highest prices that will still lead to full occupancy, it will make more money than it would if too-high prices led to unoccupied rooms or too-low prices filled the building but essentially gave money back to customers unnecessarily. Marriott introduced revenue management to the lodging industry, and over the past two decades has continued to refine its capability with the help of analytics—even as most competitors are constantly a step behind in their ability to optimize revenues.

Recent enhancements make the system work faster so that pricing could be easily and frequently adjusted for hotel rooms, and they have allowed Marriott to extend revenue management into its restaurants, catering services, and meeting spaces—an approach Marriott calls "total hotel optimization." In late 2003, the company began using a new revenue management system and began to use a new metric—revenue opportunity—that relates actual revenues to optimal revenues. In 2005, Marriott had a revenue opportunity figure of 91 percent—up from 83 percent in 2003.[1] While the company prefers its franchisees to use the system, it has given its regional "revenue leaders" the power to override the system's recommendations to deal with unanticipated local events, such as the arrival in Houston of a large number of Hurricane Katrina evacuees.

A successful revenue management system has helped Marriott achieve consistently strong financial performance. Marriott employs an enterprise-wide revenue management system called One Yield. The system automates the business processes associated with optimizing revenue for more than 1,700 of the company's 2,600 properties.

Marriott hotels that have installed One Yield have seen an increase of up to 2 percent in revenue from leisure travelers in 2004, providing an annual profit increase for individual hotels totaling $86 million. In 2003, operating income rose 17 percent, while Marriott added 185 new hotels and over 31,000 rooms, approximately one-third of which were conversions from competing hotel brands. Marriott attributes these results in part to One Yield.[2]

In addition to revenue management, Marriott has embedded analytics into several other customer-facing processes. The company has identified its most profitable customers through its Marriott Rewards loyalty program and targets marketing offers and campaigns to them.

Marriott also maintains a sophisticated Web analytics capability for its online channel, through which it did $4 billion in business last year. The Web analytics group is constantly doing tests to understand the impact of changes in its Web site. Analytics has become such a focus within sales and marketing that all analytical people were recently combined into one organizational unit. Partly as a result of Marriott's analytical prowess, the company has been named the most admired firm in its industry for seven straight years in *Fortune* magazine's ranking.

Another analytical competitor whose innovations have kept it ahead of its rivals is Progressive Insurance. Progressive's top managers relentlessly hunt for undiscovered insurance markets and business models that have been ignored by companies that perform only conventional data analysis.

Progressive was the first insurance company to offer auto insurance online in real time and the first to allow online rate comparisons—the company is so confident in its price setting that it assumes that companies offering lower rates are taking on unprofitable customers.[3] It has even pioneered a program that would offer discounts to safer drivers who voluntarily used the company's TripSensor technology to measure such factors as how often they make sudden stops and the percentage of time they drive more than 75 miles per hour.[4] By digging deeper into customer information and doing it faster and earlier than the competition, the company uncovers new opportunities and exploits them before the rest of the industry takes notice. These and other tactics have paid off handsomely, as the company's market capitalization has doubled over the past four years to $23 billion.

What do the stories of Capital One, Marriott International, and Progressive Insurance have in common? They demonstrate not only the concept of competing on analytics but also the connection between the extensive use of analytics and business performance. In this chapter, we will explore those links in greater detail and describe how several highly successful companies have transformed their ability to compete on analytics into a key point of differentiation and lasting competitive advantage.

Assessing the Evidence

Many researchers have found that fact-based decision processes are critical to high performance. In *Good to Great*, for example, Jim Collins notes that "breakthrough results come about by a series of good decisions, diligently executed and accumulated on top of another . . . [Good-to-great companies] made many more good decisions than bad ones, and they made many more good decisions than comparison companies . . . They infused the entire process with the brutal facts of reality . . . You absolutely cannot make a series of good decisions without first confronting the brutal facts."[5]

Researchers have also begun to document the returns that companies can earn from investments in specific analytical technologies or initiatives. For example, technology research firm International Data Corporation (IDC) found in one study that analytical projects aimed at improving production had a median ROI of 277 percent; those involving financial management had a median ROI of 139 percent; and those focused on customer relationship management, a median ROI of 55 percent.[6] The study also showed that the median ROI for business intelligence projects using predictive technologies was 145 percent, compared with a median ROI of 89 percent for projects without them.[7] But because the idea of competing on analytics is a new concept, academic studies do not yet exist that link a comprehensive analytical approach to business performance as a whole.

To begin to fill in the gaps of evidence about the effect of analytics on business performance, we conducted two surveys—the first an in-depth sample of thirty-two organizations that we rated in terms of their analytical orientations, and the second a much larger survey of firms that had made major investments in enterprise systems. In the first survey, we rated each firm's stage of analytical maturity (the same 5-point scale described in chapter 2, with 1 equaling major challenges to analytical competition and 5 indicating analytical mastery). Then we gathered financial performance data on all the survey participants. After conducting a statistical analysis of the data, we found a significant correlation between higher levels of analytical maturity and robust five-year compound annual growth rates.[8]

In the second study, we surveyed more than 450 executives in 371 large and medium-sized companies. We limited this study to those companies that had already implemented at least two modules of an enterprise system and therefore had a sufficient quantity and quality of transaction data available for analysis.[9] Those companies represented eighteen industries in thirty-four countries.[10] This study was a follow-up to an earlier study conducted in 2002 on the value of enterprise systems and analytics.[11]

In the large survey, we found a direct relationship between enterprise systems and decision making. For example, while many organizations initially invest in enterprise systems to improve efficiency and streamline processes, we found that cost savings were not their primary objective. In both the 2002 and 2006 studies, a majority (53 percent) of respondents identified "improved decision making" as one of their top three business objectives. To help managers make more-informed and faster decisions, organizations initially invest in enterprise systems to deliver reliable transaction-level data and "a single version of the truth"—an important precursor to developing an analytical capability. Once a firm has established a solid foundation of high-quality transaction data, its managers are able to shift their focus to using the data and systems for better decision making.

We also found that companies are becoming more analytical over time and building their commitment to analytics. In 2002 nearly half (45 percent) of the companies we surveyed reported that they had minimal or no analytical capabilities. However, four years later, only 8 percent said they lacked basic analytical capabilities.

Similarly, the number of organizations with significant or advanced analytical capabilities supported by extensive and integrated management information doubled from 28 percent to 57 percent.

Most important, we found a striking relationship between the use of analytics and business performance. When we compared the responses of high performers (those who outperformed their industry in terms of profit, shareholder return, and revenue growth—about 13 percent of the sample) with those of low performers (16 percent of the sample), we found that the majority of high-performing businesses strategically apply analytics in their daily operations. And about 10 percent of executives cited analytics as a key element of their company's strategy. High performers were 50 percent more likely to use analytics strategically compared with the overall sample and five times as likely as low performers.

Further, we discovered a significant statistical association between an organization's commitment to analytics and high performance. Companies with strong analytical orientations (those who answered with a 4 or 5 on all our questions) represented 25 percent of the sample (ninety-three companies), and their orientations correlated highly with financial outperformance in terms of profit, revenue, and shareholder return.[12] In fact, one of the strongest and most consistent differences between low- and high-performance businesses is their attitude toward,

FIGURE 3-1

Importance of analytical orientation:
high performers versus low performers, 2006

Low performers		High performers
23%	Have significant decision-support/analytical capabilities	65%
8%	Value analytical insights to a very large extent	36%
33%	Have above average analytical capability within industry	77%
23%	Use analytics across their entire organization	40%

and applications of, analytics (see figure 3-1).[13] For example, 65 percent of high performers indicated they have significant decision-support or real-time analytical capabilities versus 23 percent of low performers. Only 8 percent of low performers valued analytical insights to a very large extent compared with 36 percent of top performers. And while one-third of the low performers in our study believe that they have above-average analytical capability within their industries, 77 percent of top performers believe that. Finally, 40 percent of high performers employ analytics broadly across their entire organization, but only 23 percent of low performers do.

The breadth and consistency of the associations described earlier suggest the wisdom of investing in analytics for any organization seeking to improve performance. Furthermore, our research confirms that while relatively few companies have adopted analytics as a competitive capability, many more aspire to do so. The leaders of these companies have made the commitment to investing in analytics as a means of improving business performance.

Analytics as a Source of Competitive Advantage

Skeptics may scoff that analytics can't provide a sustainable competitive advantage, because any single insight or analysis eventually can be adopted by competitors. And it is true that an individual insight may provide only transient benefits. Yield management provided a big boost to American Airlines for a time, for example, but using that process is now just a cost of doing business in the airline industry.

Organizations can take several approaches to gain a competitive advantage with data. Some can collect unique data over time about their customers and prospects that competitors cannot match. Others can organize, standardize, and manipulate data that is available to others in a unique fashion. Still others might develop a proprietary algorithm that leads to better, more insightful analyses upon which to make decisions. And some differentiate themselves by embedding analytics into a distinctive business process.

Regardless of the approach, for companies to sustain a competitive advantage, analytics must be applied judiciously, executed well, and continually renewed. Companies that successfully compete on analytics have analytical capabilities that are:

- **Hard to duplicate.** It's one thing to copy another company's IT applications or its products and their related attributes (such as price, placement, or promotion), quite another to replicate processes and culture. For example, other banks have tried to copy Capital One's strategy of experimentation and testing, but they haven't been as successful. Banks that have been successful with a similar strategy, such as Barclays in the United Kingdom, have figured out their own route to analytical competition. While Capital One relentlessly seeks new customers, Barclays leverages analytics to increase "share of wallet" by cross-selling to its large customer base.

- **Unique.** There is no single correct path to follow to become an analytical competitor, and the way every company uses analytics is unique to its strategy and market position. For example, in the gaming industry, Harrah's uses analytics to encourage customers to play in a variety of its locations. This makes sense for Harrah's, because it has long had its casinos scattered around the United States. But that approach clearly would not be the right one for a single casino, such as Foxwoods Resort Casino in Connecticut. It's also less appealing for casino impresario Steve Wynn, who has translated his intuitive sense of style and luxury into the destination resorts Bellagio and the Wynn.

- **Adaptable to many situations.** An analytical organization can cross internal boundaries and apply analytical capabilities in innovative ways. Sprint, for example, easily adapted its analytical expertise in marketing to improve its human capital processes. The company applied its "customer experience life cycle" model to create an analogous "employee experience life cycle" model that helped it optimize employee acquisition and retention.

- **Better than the competition.** Even in industries where analytical expertise and consistent data are prevalent, some organizations are just better at exploiting information than others. While every financial services firm has access to the consumer risk information from FICO, for example, Capital One has analytical skills and knowledge that enables it to outperform the market by making smarter decisions about potentially risky credit customers. The company's managers refer to the concept of *deaveraging*— how can they break apart a category or a metric to get more analytical advantage?

- **Renewable.** Any competitive advantage needs to be a moving target, with continued improvement and reinvestment. Analytics are particularly well suited to continuous innovation and renewal. Progressive Insurance, for example, describes its competitive advantage in terms of the agility it gains through a disciplined analytical approach. By the time competitors notice that Progressive has targeted a new segment—such as older motorcycle drivers—it has captured the market and moved on to the next opportunity. In its 2005 annual report, the company described its ongoing commitment to develop and exploit new insights in understated fashion: "Our knowledge of the calculus combining price, growth and profit, while increasing, remains a challenge and something we want to be smart about."[14]

One caveat: companies in heavily regulated industries, or in those for which the availability of data is limited, will be constrained from exploiting analytics to the fullest. For example, outside the United States, pharmaceutical firms are prevented from obtaining data about prescriptions from individual physicians. As a result, pharmaceutical marketing activities in other parts of the world are generally much less analytical than those of companies selling in the U.S. market. But in other cases, analytics can permanently transform an industry or process. As *Moneyball* and *Liar's Poker* author Michael Lewis points out in talking about investment banking, "The introduction of derivatives and other new financial instruments brought unprecedented levels of complexity and variation to investment firms. The old-school, instinct guys who knew when to buy and when to sell were watching young MBAs—or worse, PhDs from MIT—bring an unprecedented level of analysis and brain power to trading. Within 10 years, the old guard was gone."[15]

Analytics in Government

We haven't written much thus far about analytics in government, because our focus in this book is on how organizations compete—and governmental organizations don't do that in the conventional sense of the term. The one area in which national governments do compete is war, and it's probably not surprising that the earliest uses of analytics in government involved national defense. The first computers were developed to calculate things like missile trajectories, and Robert McNamara introduced a broad range of analytical approaches to the military—not always with success—when he was secretary of defense in the 1960s. In the present military environment, analytics are used extensively for military intelligence, including automated analysis of text and voice communications (sometimes to considerable public controversy).

Today, however, analytics are widely used at many levels of government, from local to state to federal. They may not necessarily increase governments' abilities to compete, but they can certainly make governments substantially more efficient and effective. At the local level, for example, perhaps the most impressive accomplishment from analytics has been the use of crime statistics analysis to deter criminals. In New York City, the CompStat program associates crimes with particular geographical regions of the city and is used to guide decisions about where police officers should be stationed. It is also linked with an effort to push decisions down to the precinct level. CompStat has been widely praised for contributing to the reduction in crime in New York since its inception. However, several other factors changed during the same time, so it is difficult to isolate CompStat's effects alone.[16]

At the state level, there are many possible analytical applications, some of which can amount to substantial savings when pursued effectively. Several states, including Massachusetts, have pursued revenue optimization approaches that have yielded hundreds of millions of dollars. These apply to tax and nontax payments. States have also pursued fraud detection to reduce improper payments for welfare, purchase cards, Medicare, and Medicaid. State departments of natural resources have used analytical approaches to model and optimize resources such as minerals, gas and oil, and parks.

At the federal level of government in the United States, one of the earliest nondefense applications of analytics was in taxpayer compliance. The Internal Revenue Service (IRS) initiated the Taxpayer Compliance Measurement Program in 1963 to analyze which taxpayers were likely to be cheating on their taxes and to close the "tax gap" between what is paid and what should be.[17] It was an effective program for the IRS, but data gathering was judged too expensive and invasive and was discontinued in 1988. The IRS continues, however, to use programs for analyzing compliance and for identifying returns to audit.

One of the most important applications of analytics in government involves health care. This is a major expense for the federal government—its largest nondefense category of spending. Medicare and Medicaid are paid for by the U.S. government but are administered by states. A large medical program that is run at the federal level is the Department of Veterans Affairs (VA) hospitals. The VA has employed electronic medical records and analytics based upon them to become one of the most effective health care providers in the United States. As a *Business Week* article about the VA hospitals titled "The Best Medical Care in the U.S." described, "In the mid-1990s, Dr. Kenneth W. Kizer, then the VA's Health Under Secretary, installed the most extensive electronic medical records system in the U.S. Kizer also decentralized decision-making, closed underused hospitals, reallocated resources, and most critically, instituted a culture of accountability and quality measurements."[18]

The VA hospitals employ such analytical approaches as predictive modeling of chronic disease, evidence-based medicine, automated decisions for treatment protocols and drug prescriptions, and many others. The VA's experience is one of the best indications that analytics can have as much of an effect on government as on the private sector.

Governments around the world are increasingly adopting predictive analytics. In the United Kingdom, for example, a police analysis uncovered the fact that 50 percent of British crimes are committed by 5 percent of criminals. As Paddy Tomkins, chief constable of Lothian and Borders in the United Kingdom, explains, "We want to exert less effort on investigating each individual crime and more on understanding the criminals . . . This will bring a disproportionate benefit for preventing crime altogether."[19]

Serving the Market for Analytical Products and Services

While our focus in this book is on how companies can use analytics to optimize key business processes, there is another way to profit from analytics: by making available analytical products or services directly to customers—either as a stand-alone offering or to augment other products and services. For companies in a position to consider this an option, we take a brief detour here.

Perhaps the best-known company that augments its offerings with analytics is Google. In addition to providing analytics for searching, which we discuss in chapter 4, and to advertisers, which we describe in chapter 5, Google makes analytics available as a service to anyone with a Web site. It acquired a Web analytics business in 2005 and renamed it Google Analytics. The company offers Google Analytics with a unique business model: it gives the service away for free. Google's goal in offering the analytical service is to improve the understanding of the Web and the Internet by providing metrics on Web site results and user behavior. Rather than competing with other Web analytics vendors, Google seeks to "lift all boats" and educate Web publishers and advertisers on whether their efforts are working and how to profit from this relatively new channel. The more people who use Web analytics well, the better the overall Web experience will be, and Google will profit in the long run. Google even provides an online Conversion University to teach the basic principles of Web analytics, in addition to publishing a blog and online articles, offering Webinars, and providing public speakers on Web analytics.

The move to analytics has also been reflected in the rise of consulting. Accenture and some other firms have identified analytical consulting as a growth area in response to client demands. Accenture's consultants, for example, help clients address the broad strategic issues around building an analytical capability, or provide assistance building and supporting a particular business initiative (e.g., a customer loyalty program). Accenture frequently tailors solutions for specific industries, such as automated underwriting in financial services. Quantitatively oriented consultants specialize in analytically intensive business solutions, such as supply chain optimization, while specialists in information management help clients develop a robust analytical technical environment. Consultants with particular industry and functional specialties (e.g., marketing or supply chain) work closely with clients while those with purely technical or statistical skills are increasingly based off-shore, particularly in India.

There are many other smaller companies with analytical offerings, and unlike Google they tend to charge for their services. Consider Apex Management Group, a company that sells actuarial and risk management information to health care insurers. It uses predictive models to identify patients at risk and, once they have been identified, to set them up with disease management programs. The company continues to roll out new offerings based on its proprietary predictive modeling and forecasting tools. In 2005, for example, Apex introduced a new capability that enables employers to assess the cost-effectiveness of different disease management programs.

Another firm whose primary business is analytics is the quantitative stock selector Franklin Portfolio Associates (a unit of Mellon Corporation). Like other "quant" firms, Franklin Portfolio uses proprietary quantitative metrics and algorithms to evaluate more than four thousand securities. The firm's computers create a list of "buy" candidates from the top four hundred securities and then use a portfolio optimizer and risk management application to select a portfolio. It has its own direct clients but also manages more than $9 billion in assets for Vanguard. Investors are increasingly turning to quantitatively managed investments. Such funds were first launched in the 1970s but have proliferated recently as fund companies seek better performance at lower cost.[20]

Sometimes firms in analytical businesses take on related tasks, such as data management and consulting. In the retail sector, Dunnhumby worked closely with Tesco on the development of the giant grocery retailer's loyalty program Clubcard, an important tool in that firm's ability to use data to optimize its product mix (for more on Tesco, see chapter 5). Catalina Marketing also sells analytical services to the grocery industry that help it understand the effects of coupons and other promotions. The firm retrieves about 250 million transactions per week from more than 21,000 grocery stores. On behalf of those stores, Catalina manages one of the largest databases in the world, containing the purchase histories of over 100 million households.[21] The company aggregates information about purchase behavior and customer demographics, attitudes, and preferences and sells that information to grocery store chains. Catalina claims that its analytically based approach can increase a company's average coupon-redemption rates up to ten times higher than they would be with traditional promotion methods.

In many cases, selling data is not enough. Companies also need help interpreting and using the data, and hence buy consulting from external providers. Information Resources Inc. (IRI), for example, has long gathered data from retailers' point-of-sale terminals, from panels of almost 100,000 consumers, and from pantry audits to understand consumption patterns. More recently, however, IRI has grown its ability to help firms in the consumer packaged goods, retail, and pharmaceutical sectors analyze data to make smarter and more profitable marketing decisions. Sunil Garga, who heads the company's Analytic Insights group, argues that because of the rise of analytics, "Marketing has changed more in the last 24 months than it has in the last 24 years, and that rate of change will continue. It's an analytic revolution."[22]

Even analytical software providers often need to provide highly customized consulting, as this discussion of services from ProfitLogic's (a retail pricing analytics firm now owned by Oracle) CEO suggests:

> What we did for massive client databases could only be described as an art—we couldn't follow a standardized formula for this type of problem solving. And, with a cadre of Harvard and MIT Ph.D.s on our payroll, our clients paid for us to solve very specific problems that couldn't be cracked by anyone else. The scientists formed the basis of our competitive differentiation since no one else in the market had the same caliber of staff. Once we sold a project it required a large investment of our scientists' time to unravel the data and develop a model . . . Our experience working with client data taught us that our models required regular fine-tuning in order to achieve sufficient accuracy.[23]

In the case of firms that sell data and analytics, the challenge is often to convince customers of the need for analytical capabilities. According to the managers we interviewed in these firms, a lack of understanding of the analytical methods and what they can accomplish, not cost, is the chief objection. This is one of the reasons why Google has taken such an evangelical and educational approach to Web analytics with its Google Analytics offering.

In a variation of the "selling analytics" approach, many established companies are finding innovative ways to enhance physical products by incorporating analytics. For example, medical products companies are designing products with sensors so that an individual's health data can be analyzed remotely rather than at a clinic or hospital. Also on the horizon are copiers that can transmit data that allows the service provider to schedule preventive maintenance and avoid downtime. And washing machines in the near future will be able to "listen" to sensors embedded inside the clothes in order to determine the right temperature setting.

Analytical products are even coming to golf, a sport that has not been a stranger to technological innovation in the past few decades. Pennsylvania-based VisViva Golf Inc.'s hardware and software makes golf clubs with embedded swing analytics. The clubs use nanotechnology that's connected to a Bluetooth radio and installed into the heads of customized clubs (drivers, wedges, and putters). Once installed, the combination of the wireless hardware in the clubs and predictive software that runs on a Windows-based PC or PDA provides golfers with the help they need to improve their swing. For example, the software in a VisViva putter instantly analyzes the back and forward strokes, displays them on a screen, and informs the golfer whether he accelerated the club, decelerated, or held the stroke speed constant. The data can also be uploaded to a golf club designer's software, and the designer can turn the data into a set of custom clubs that are perfectly matched to the golfer's swing.[24]

When Analytics Aren't Enough

We wish we could argue that using analytics well is all an organization needs to improve business performance. But there are good examples that disprove that assertion. Large U.S. airlines, such as American and United, are exhibit A. They are analytical competitors but not very successful. Both airlines (American a bit more than United) were pioneers in adopting such analytical approaches as yield management for seat pricing, optimization of routes and resource scheduling, and the analysis of loyalty program data. While we believe that these companies would be worse off without their use of analytics, neither has fared particularly well. United has spent most of the last decade in bankruptcy, and American has barely stayed out of it.

What happened? Two things have kept these firms from succeeding with their analytical strategies. One is that their analytics support an obsolete business model. They pioneered analytics for yield management, but other airlines with lower costs can still offer lower prices (on average, if not for a particular seat). They pioneered analytics for complex optimization of routes with many different airplane types, but competitors such as Southwest save both money and complexity by using only one type of plane. They pioneered loyalty programs and promotions based on data analysis, but their customer service is so indifferent that loyalty to these airlines is difficult for frequent flyers.

The other problem with their analytical approaches is that other airlines have adopted them. Even discount carriers such as Southwest and JetBlue make diligent use of yield management and crew-scheduling analytics. If the discounters lack internal capabilities for analytics, they can buy them from providers such as Navitaire (and Sabre Airline Solutions, which used to be part of American but has now been spun out as a separate company). Industry data is widely available from associations and external providers to any airline that wants to analyze it. In short, there are virtually no barriers preventing any airline from employing standard analytical approaches, and an airline would have to work very hard to distinguish itself in analytical competition at this point. Perhaps other frontiers of analytical orientation will emerge in that industry in the future.

Conclusion

The success of companies like Capital One, Marriott, Progressive, and Google demonstrates that the use of analytics can lead to better business performance and, indeed, competitive advantage. While academic work remains to be done to quantify the benefits of this still-new way of doing business, preliminary research indicates that individual analytical projects pay major dividends, and survey data confirms that analytical approaches are correlated with high performance. We have also identified five factors that make an analytical approach a source of competitive advantage. In the next two chapters, we'll explore in more detail how certain companies are using analytics to outperform the competition. Chapter 4 addresses internal processes, and chapter 5 deals with external processes, such as those involving customers and suppliers.

4

COMPETING ON ANALYTICS
WITH INTERNAL PROCESSES

Financial, Manufacturing, R&D,
and Human Resource Applications

ANALYTICS CAN BE APPLIED TO many business processes to gain a competitive edge. We've divided the world of analytical support for business processes into two categories: internal and external. The next chapter will address external applications—customer- and supplier-driven processes—and this one will focus on internal applications (refer to figure 4-1). It's not always a perfectly clean distinction; in this chapter, for example, the internal applications sometimes involve external data and entities, even though they are not primarily about supply and demand, customers, or supply chains. But the focus here is on such internally facing functions as general management, finance and accounting, R&D, manufacturing, and human resource management. These are, in fact, the earliest applications of "decision support." The original intent was that this data and these systems would be used to manage the business internally. Only more recently have they been applied to working with customers and suppliers, as companies have accumulated better data about the outside world with which they interact.

The challenge, then, is not simply to identify internal applications of business analytics but to find some that are clearly strategic and involve competitive advantage. Any company, for example, can have a financial or operational scorecard, but how does it contribute to a distinctive,

FIGURE 4-1

Application domains for analytics

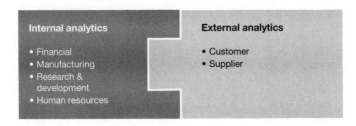

strategic capability? Customer-related applications are more likely to be strategic almost by definition; internal applications have to work at it to make a strategic impact. They have to lead to measurable improvements to financial or operational performance. In the box "Typical Analytical Applications for Internal Processes," we list some common approaches.

Typical Analytical Applications for Internal Processes

Activity-based costing (ABC). The first step in activity-based management is to allocate costs accurately to aspects of the business such as customers, processes, or distribution channels; models incorporating activities, materials, resources, and product-offering components then allow optimization based on cost and prediction of capacity needs.

Bayesian inference (e.g., to predict revenues). A numerical estimate of the degree of belief in a hypothesis before and after evidence has been observed.

Biosimulation (e.g., in pharmaceutical "in silico" research). Manipulation of biological parameters using mathematics and/or rule bases to model how cells or other living entities react to chemical or other interventions.

Combinatorial optimization (e.g., for optimizing a product portfolio). The efficient allocation of limited resources to yield the best solution to particular objectives when the values of some or all of the variables (e.g., a given number of people) must be integers (because people can't be split into fractions) and there are many possible combinations. Also called *integer programming.*

Constraint analysis (e.g., for product configuration). The use of one or more constraint satisfaction algorithms to specify the set of feasible solutions. Constraints are programmed in rules or procedures that produce solutions to particular configuration and design problems using one or more constraint satisfaction algorithms.

Experimental design (e.g., for Web site analysis). In the simplest type of experiment, participants are randomly assigned to two groups that are equivalent to each other. One group (the program or treatment group) gets the program and the other group (the comparison or control group) does not. If the program results in statistically significant differences in the outcome variable, it is assumed to have the hypothesized effect.

Future-value analysis. The decomposition of market capitalization into current value (extrapolation of existing monetary returns) and future value, or expectations of future growth.

Monte Carlo simulation (e.g., for R&D project valuation). A computerized technique used to assess the probability of certain outcomes or risks by mathematically modeling a hypothetical event over multiple trials and comparing the outcome with predefined probability distributions.

Multiple regression analysis (e.g., to determine how nonfinancial factors affect financial performance). A statistical technique whereby the influence of a set of independent variables on a single dependent variable is determined.

Neural network analysis (e.g., to predict the onset of disease). Systems modeled on the structure and operation of the brain, in which the state of the system is modified by training until it can discriminate between the classes of inputs; used on large databases. Typically, a neural network is initially "trained," or fed large amounts of data and rules about data relationships—for example, "A grandfather is older than a person's father."

Textual analysis (e.g., to assess intangible capabilities). Analysis of the frequency, semantic relationships, and relative importance of particular terms, phrases, and documents in online text.

Yield analysis (e.g., in semiconductor manufacturing). Employing basic statistics (mean, median, standard deviation, etc.) to understand yield volume and quality, and to compare one batch of items with another—often displayed visually.

Financial Analytics

We'll start by discussing financial applications, since they of course have the most direct tie to financial performance. There are several categories of financial analytics applications, including external reporting, *enterprise performance management* (management reporting and scorecards), investment decisions, shareholder value analysis, and cost management.

External Reporting to Regulatory Bodies and Shareholders

External reporting doesn't lead to competitive advantage under "business as usual" conditions. It's not normally an advantage to report more quickly and accurately beyond a certain level. Cisco Systems, for example, has touted over the last several years its ability to close the books instantaneously and to report its results almost immediately at the end of a financial period. But we often wondered why it bothered; the SEC doesn't demand instantaneous closes, and it's not clear what else a company could do with financial results intended for external consumption. But it is a different story with the information used by managers to make better strategic, investment, and operational decisions.

Reporting and scorecards, both financial and operational, are some of the most common applications of business intelligence and decision support. They're obviously important to managing any business, and they're increasingly important (with the advent of Sarbanes-Oxley legislation, for example) to keeping senior executives out of jail. While organizations do not compete on the basis of their reporting and scorecards, having systems in place to monitor progress against key operating metrics and monitor progress against plan is critical to strategy execution.[1] As we argued in chapter 1, reporting activities have typically not made extensive use of analytics, but there are exceptions. One is the prediction of future performance.

Public companies have to make regular predictions of future performance for investors and analysts. The consequences of poor predictions can be dramatic; investors may severely punish companies that fail to "meet their numbers." Most companies make straightforward extrapolations of results from earlier periods to later ones. Yet in certain industries with a high degree of change and uncertainty, extrapolations can be problematic and yield poor predictions.

The information technology industry is one of those uncertain industries. Products and customer desires change rapidly, and disproportionate sales volumes take place at the ends of reporting periods. Hewlett-Packard (HP) found that it was very difficult to make accurate predictions of revenues in such an environment, and in one quarter of 2001 had a "nearly disastrous" revenue growth forecasting error of 12 percent.[2] HP executives decided to put some of their quantitative researchers in HP Labs onto the problem of creating more accurate revenue forecasts.

The researchers used a Bayesian inference approach (see the box) to predict monthly and quarterly revenues from data thus far in the period. After several adjustments, the algorithm yielded significantly better revenue predictions than the more straightforward approach used previously. HP incorporated the new algorithm into its performance-reporting dashboard, and the company's (then) CFO, Bob Wayman, noted, "It is reassuring to have a solid projection algorithm. It's crisper and cleaner, it has rigor and methodology as opposed to my own algorithm."[3]

Better prediction of future performance from an operational standpoint also allows companies to take action sooner. Using "near-real-time" operational data, managers can quickly identify emerging trends, make predictions, and take prompt action. For example, during the last recession, Dell executives used predictive models to recognize months before their competitors how thoroughly sales were going to soften. They took preemptive action on prices and products, which resulted in better (or at least, less awful) financial performance during the downturn. More importantly, as the recession ended, they were able to adjust again to boost their market share.

Enterprise Performance Management and Scorecards

Another exception to financial-reporting applications involving analytics is when companies try to explain financial performance from nonfinancial factors. A successful enterprise performance management initiative requires companies not just to predict performance accurately but also to come to grips with some broader questions: Which activities have the greatest impact on business performance? How do we know whether we are executing against our strategy? An organization needs quantifiable insight into the operational factors that contribute to business results and a way of measuring progress against them.

Over the past decade or so, the biggest advance in management re-porting has been the adoption of management dashboards or balanced scorecards. These scorecards report not only on financial performance but also on such nonfinancial domains as customer relationships, em-ployee learning and innovation, and operations. These have been a great step forward in understanding performance. But most adopters of balanced scorecards aren't very balanced, focusing primarily on finan-cial reporting. It's great to add nonfinancial metrics to a scorecard, but if investors and regulators don't really care about them, it's natural to emphasize the financial numbers.

Another problem with most scorecards is that even when compa-nies do have both financial and nonfinancial measures in their score-cards, they don't relate them to each other. Management professors David Larcker and Chris Ittner studied several companies that had adopted balanced scorecards.[4] None of the companies they examined had causal models that related nonfinancial to financial performance.

Nonfinancial or intangible resources (such as human knowledge capital, brand, and R&D capability) are growing in importance to both company business performance and external perceptions of company value.[5] Even the most favorable studies only show an explanatory power of approximately 50 percent for the effect of financial measures such as earnings per share, net income, economic profit, or return on invested capital on a company's market value.[6] In some industries, EPS accounts for less than 5 percent of value. We believe that a management team that manages all its sources of value—tangible and intangible, current and future—has a significant advantage over those who do not.

Some companies are working to develop a holistic understanding of both financial and nonfinancial value drivers. A few companies at the frontier are seeking to manage both their current and future share-holder value.[7] These organizations are exploring how to infuse their scorecards with data from Wall Street analysts and future-value analyt-ics to gain better insight into the implications of decisions on share-holder value. Companies that develop such a capability might be well on the way to competitive advantage.

Reporting and scorecards are most likely to lead to competitive ad-vantage when the business environment is changing dramatically. In those circumstances, it's particularly important to monitor new forms of performance. New measures need to be developed, new models of performance need to be created, and new management behaviors need to emerge. The speed and effectiveness of organizational transformation in such periods can certainly be or lead to a competitive advantage. For example, a property and casualty insurance company we worked with needed to transform itself. It was a poor financial performer, with losses over the last four years of well over a billion dollars. It paid out $1.40 in claims and expenses for every premium dollar it took in. The company had monitored its financial results, but it didn't have a handle on what was creating the poor performance.

As part of a major corporate transformation, the company focused on three key processes: producer (agent) relationships, profitable underwriting, and claims execution. In addition to redesigning those processes, the company created new measures of them and collected them in a balanced scorecard. The scorecard served as a means to rapidly communicate the performance of and changes in the processes, and the success of the change initiative overall, to the management team. The scorecard assessed the company's ability to deliver on such objectives as:

- Selecting profitable new markets to enter
- Attracting and selecting the right customers
- Driving pricing in accordance with risk
- Reducing the severity of claims

Reward systems for employees and managers at all levels of the company were changed to tie to performance on these objectives. Some automated analytics were embedded into underwriting systems to speed the process and improve the quality of pricing decisions.

The company used these process changes and reporting approaches to dramatically turn itself around. It began to make substantial amounts of profit and was eventually acquired by another insurance firm for $3.5 billion—up from perhaps zero value a few years earlier.

A medium-sized semiconductor firm is similarly undergoing a major corporate transformation today. The company has historically been driven by its engineering capabilities and has sold to customers what it could design and manufacture. Today, however, its executives have concluded that it needs to change its capabilities to focus on marketing and customer relationships. The entire industry is changing, and market leaders such as Intel have concluded that identifying markets and applications for semiconductors (such as mobile computing and multimedia technology) is more important than squeezing a few more MIPS out of microprocessors.

The alternative is to understand markets and customers better and to begin to serve the most profitable customers. In the past, the company had worked diligently to satisfy customers even if doing so wasn't even profitable. Now new metrics of customer profitability have been developed, and both customer-facing personnel and management are being measured on this criterion. Like the insurance company, the semiconductor firm is putting its new measures in a balanced scorecard and has developed "strategy maps" that link the new measures and reporting structures to its new strategy. The new reporting approach has only recently been adopted, but virtually every senior manager believes that if the company is to compete and prosper in this new competitive environment, the new reporting system will be a critical component.

Cost Management

Although some might question whether cost management can lead to a competitive advantage, there are an increasing number of examples of firms that have made effective analysis and management of costs a strategic capability. In some cases the new insights into costs are applied for internal management only; in others they are used to help set the prices that customers pay and the customer behaviors that companies attempt to influence. We'll give one example of each type. Cost allocation is not in itself a highly analytical activity, but once completed, it allows the optimization of costs through modeling and rapid, accurate decisions about how business relationships and pricing should be treated. For example, it can be used to decide which distribution channel a particular customer should be encouraged to use and what price she should be charged.

One of the pressing reasons for managing costs well is when a bankruptcy court judge orders you to do so. That was the situation faced by MCI, which went into bankruptcy because of poor (and at times illegal, according to the courts) financial management when the company was known as WorldCom. One of the company's problems was that it had little or no control or even awareness of its product/service costs. Various services were offered over the customer's networks, but there was little sense of the resources and costs necessary to make those services available. Under these conditions, it was easy to view the company's revenue as purely incremental, with no costs—and if people think things are free, they are often priced too low. The company had many revenue reports but very few relating to costs. As a result, it was impossible to determine the profitability of offerings to customers.

This revenue orientation may have been reasonable at one time, but today the telecommunications business has become more commoditized. It's harder to grow your way into profitability. So MCI embarked upon a major initiative to calculate its activity-based costs. It created 5,000 cost centers, grouped into 970 cost groups. A set of costing factors (business versus consumer focus, for example) was created to apply to each of the cost centers each month. The costing factors are reviewed annually. MCI created a collection point for the cost information at the enterprise level, which was much more effective than the previous approach. As John Nolan, MCI's vice president for analysis and planning, put it, "We used to try to line up data fields from 300 spreadsheets. When we started using an activity-based costing tool, there were tears of joy about what this tool could do."[8]

As with many other major analytical initiatives, there was considerable support from MCI's senior management for the cost management initiative. Mike Capellas, MCI's CEO at the time, had been known for a strong data orientation at Compaq, which he had previously headed. He believed strongly in allocating all costs to P&Ls. At MCI he consistently championed the costing effort, and he publicized his preferences by refusing to look at any P&L without fully allocated costs. The cost and profitability information at MCI is now being used to determine compensation, and has begun to change management behavior and refocus attention.

Most importantly, the cost information allowed MCI to understand the profitability of its service offerings and customer segments, which was a condition of emerging from bankruptcy. The new focus on profitability impressed Wall Street, which consequently valued MCI's equity more highly. In 2005, MCI was sold to Verizon for a price of $8.4 billion, and there is little doubt that the cost analytics helped increase the value of the company.[9]

For an example of cost management involving customers (i.e., still an example of internal use of analytics but with external benefit), we can turn to RBC Financial Group, whose major business unit is better known as Royal Bank of Canada—the largest bank in that country. RBC wasn't losing money or in bankruptcy court, but around the year 2000, a couple of senior executives and an IT manager determined that they could make substantially more money if they achieved a better understanding of customer profitability. Doing so would allow the bank to understand which customers were profitable, which services ought to be offered to which customers, and how unprofitable customers might be turned into profitable ones.

RBC had some advantages in customer profitability analytics. The company had long been customer focused. As early as the late 1970s, a visionary started a customer information file—a universal customer record for retail and commercial banking—that contained information on all of the bank's products. There was even a customer profitability model, which had been built in 1992. The problem was that it wasn't very accurate. It used aggregate information, rather than individual customer data, to place customers into three different profitability groups. According to Kevin Purkiss, RBC's senior vice president of client profitability analytics:

> The model placed customers into three large "buckets:" A, B and C. The "A" customers made the most profit, the "B" customers made some, and the "C" customers broke even or lost money. This information was delivered to the field office. It helped align the sales force around customer profitability and planted the seeds for the new customer-centric organization. However, it wasn't refined enough for advanced channel optimization or relationship pricing. In addition, we realized later that in some instances, customers were treated without consideration of the potential business they could contribute.[10]

Before it could create a better customer profitability model, RBC first needed better information on its costs. The bank had employed activity-based costing for over twenty-five years, but until the late 1990s, it wasn't able to assign costs to customer service channels such as tellers, ATMs, and telephone banking. At that point a new initiative was undertaken to identify the costs of those channels, as Chitwant Kohli, vice president of costing and profitability (to even have such a role is unusual) explained:

> As a services company, we are most interested in tracking labor costs, which make up over 60 percent of non-interest expenses. We extract expense data quarterly from the general ledger for each individual cost cen-

ter. These cost centers are then grouped with like units based on the products, services, and activities performed by the unit . . . For example, domestic branches, which sell and service the same product lines using the same processes, became a unit group . . . Within the 30 to 40 unit type groups, we establish total staff time consumed by each activity based on unit time per activity multiplied by volumes processed. This enables the proper allocation of the unit's salary cost to products and activities and also forms the basis for apportioning premises and general operating costs. Once we have these drivers by product, activity, and channel, we can aggregate costs across all units to arrive at both transaction and total product cost. These costs are then available for use in profitability models. For example, we can report the full end-to-end product cost of residential mortgages including acquisition and renewal costs by channel, back office processing, call center support, system costs, Head Office and regional overheads. For every customer we can then arrive at the costs associated with "ownership" of each separate product in the customer's portfolio, based on transaction usage and channel preference.[11]

While the math to compute activity-based costs isn't that difficult, coming up with the needed data does require a substantial degree of diligent investigation. In RBC's case, however, it clearly was worth the trouble. The bank could use this cost information to assign costs to the different products, channels, and transaction types that customers use, and from that could determine the transaction and lifetime projected profitability of customers. RBC now feels that it has high-quality customer profitability information models and no longer needs to refine the data or the models. Instead, the focus is on how the information is used, according to Kevin Purkiss: "For us, ongoing competition is based on how you use the information. At this point rather than refining the model, we get more bang for the buck out of how we can use the information in our business. We've done lots of work on value propositions— trying to understand different segments and how they relate to product lines and new products. We gained lots of insight on that two years ago, and now we're trying to better understand geographical variations."[12]

Purkiss feels that today about 10 percent of large banks have ABC and profitability information, so it is less of a competitive advantage than it was when RBC did it around the year 2000. However, most banks have not employed these analytics across all products, services, and geographies, as RBC has largely done by this point. The barriers to doing so are perhaps less technological and more organizational, and are part of taking an enterprise-wide approach to analytics.

Merger and Acquisition Analytics

Mergers and acquisitions (M&A) have historically not been the focus of a lot of analytical activity, perhaps with the exception of detailed cash flow analyses. There is usually little attention to operational analytics involving supply chain efficiencies, predicted customer reactions, and impacts on costs within the combined organization. This may be a reason why a high proportion—estimates as high as 70 and 80 percent—of M&A deals are not terribly successful in terms of producing economic value.

It doesn't have to be that way, however. Certainly some M&A deals must be done so quickly that extensive analytics would be difficult or impossible. When Bank of America was given the opportunity to acquire Fleet Bank, for example, it had about forty-eight hours to make a decision. But for most deals, there's plenty of time to undertake analyses. At Procter & Gamble, for example, the acquisition of Gillette was considered for more than a year before the deal was announced. P&G's analysis identified significant savings (in its supply chain, through workforce reductions and potential gains from customer synergies), which were used to determine how much P&G offered for Gillette in the deal. Similarly, CEMEX, the global cement company, uses analytics to quantify expected benefits from increased market share and improved profitability by enforcing its processes and systems on the takeover target.

Manufacturing, Operations, and Quality Analytics

One analytical domain that has long existed in companies is operations, especially manufacturing and quality. This was the original home, for example, of Total Quality Management and Six Sigma, which, when done seriously, involve detailed statistical analysis of process variations, defect rates, and sources of problems. Manufacturing and quality analytics have had an enormous impact on the global manufacturing industries, but their impact has been less revolutionary for service industries and nonmanufacturing functions within manufacturing companies. For the great majority of organizations, it seems difficult to summon the required levels of discipline and rigor to apply statistical quality control or even a strong process orientation outside of manufacturing. This means, of course, that it becomes difficult for firms to compete broadly on the basis of analytics, since they are often limited to the manufacturing function and generally focused on achieving productivity improvements rather than innovations to gain a competitive advantage.

Real analytical competitors in manufacturing, then, are those that go beyond just manufacturing. There are a few great examples of this approach. One is at a small steel manufacturer in the United States, and it illustrates that analytical competition applies both to smaller firms and to the manufacture of commodity goods. Rocky Mountain Steel Mills, a steel rail-, rod-, and bar-making division of Oregon Steel, faced a critical decision about manufacturing capacity in early 2005. It had shut down its seamless pipe mill in 2003 because of price pressures, but the primary customers for seamless pipe were oil drillers, and by 2005 oil prices had risen enough to make Rob Simon, the company's vice president and general manager, consider reopening the pipe mill. However, he found the rules of thumb and standard costing/volume analyses previously used for such decisions to be too simplistic for a fast-changing mix of demand, pricing, production constraints, and industry capacity.

Simon decided to turn to a more analytical approach, and Rocky Mountain installed an analytical software tool called Profit InSight. He began to work with monthly analyses to determine whether the plant should be reopened. Potential customers and other managers thought that the high prices for pipe clearly justified the capital outlay that would be needed to reopen, but Simon's analyses suggested that increased revenues for pipe would be offset by lower production of rod and bar, and would not be profitable. Only when pipe prices continued to rise throughout 2005 did Simon decide to reopen the plant in December of that year. Even when production started, his models suggested holding off on taking orders because prices were predicted to rise. Indeed, by January 2006 they had risen by 20 percent over the previous quarter.

Rocky Mountain estimates that in addition to the higher prices it received, it averted a $34 million loss it would have faced from production constraints had it reopened the plant earlier in 2005. The success with the new pipe mill was also a key factor in a substantial rise in Oregon Steel's stock price. Profit InSight is now used as a weekly strategic planning tool, and Rocky Mountain Steel Mills has completely abandoned its previous "rhetorical" sales planning and forecasting approach for the new analytical methods. They are measurably superior, but Simon still had to demand that everyone listen to what the analyses show and quit second-guessing using the old approaches.

Analytics can also be applied to assess manufactured quality. Honda, for example, has long been known for the quality of its automobiles and other products. The company certainly has analytical individuals in its manufacturing quality department. However, it goes well beyond that function in identifying potential quality problems. Honda instituted an analytical "early warning" program to identify major potential quality issues from warranty service records. These records are sent to Honda by dealers, and they include both categorized quality problems and free text. Other text comes from transcripts of calls by mechanics to experts in various domains at headquarters and from customer calls to call centers. Honda's primary concern was that any serious problems identified by dealers or customers would be noticed at headquarters and addressed quickly. So Honda analysts set up a system to mine the textual data coming from these different sources. Words appearing for the first time (particularly those suggesting major problems, such as *fire*) and words appearing more than predicted were flagged for human analysts to look at. Honda won't go into details about any specific problems it's nipped in the bud, but says that the program has been very successful.

Toshiba Semiconductor Company is another business that has made extensive use of analytics—in particular, visual representation of statistical analysis—in manufacturing quality. The initial applications focused on advanced analysis for new product and technology development, but they expanded quickly into other areas such as sales, marketing, development, production, and quality assurance. The company's executives are strong advocates of analytics, and have led the company by the concept for over six years. The overall approach at Toshiba is encompassed by a broader initiative entitled "Management Innovation Policy and Activity."

The visual analytics approach was first used by engineers in several semiconductor fabrication plants (fabs) for yield analysis—a key problem in the industry. According to Shigeru Komatsu, the company's Chief Knowledge Officer (it is rare for analytics be addressed in such a role, but they are at Toshiba Semiconductor), "We have worked on standardizing performance indicators, we have built shared databases, we have made efforts to share analysis cases and results, and we have implemented analytic software such as Minitab and Spotfire DecisionSite in order to increase our efficiency in analytics."[13]

One key issue with analytics in manufacturing is how well production workers can actually use sophisticated analytical tools, but Toshiba has found that visual analytics help to address this problem. "We observed that only 20 percent of the possible users of yield management software, for example, actually use it effectively. This is not only because the complicated special features make it hard to use for many engineers, but also because it only has a part of the data we need to analyze," said Koji Kimura, the yield manager at Toshiba's bipolar fab in Kitakyushu.[14] Using the visual approach, Toshiba has been able to take an integrated approach to analytics in its business. The company combines analytics with a highly disciplined approach to quality and both operational and managerial innovation.

Another key aspect of manufacturing analytics is to ensure that the right products are being manufactured. We'll refer to it as the *configuration problem*—making sure that the products offered to the market are those that the market wants. The configuration problem, like the ones described earlier, is cross-functional; it takes place at the intersection of sales and manufacturing, and usually also involves the supply chain, financial, and even human resource processes of the company. To compete on the basis of configuration is thus by definition an enterprise-wide activity. Configuration is highly analytical. It involves predictive modeling of what customers want to buy, as well as complex (usually rule-based) analysis of what components go with what other components into what finished products.

What companies compete on the basis of configuration? Some high-technology companies, such as Dell, are known for their configurable products. Wireless telecommunications companies may have many different service plans; some have developed automated analytical applications to find the best one for each customer. They also tailor their services to each corporate account. Automobile companies need to compete on configuration, though U.S. and European manufacturers have traditionally done it poorly. Since manufacturing a car from scratch to a customer's specification is viewed as taking too long (at least outside of Japan, where it is commonly done), car companies have to forecast the types of vehicles and options customers will want, manufacture them, and send them to dealers. Far too often, the mixes of models and option packages have not been what customers want, so cars have to be substantially discounted to be sold during promotions or at the end of a model year. The mismatch between consumer desires and available product has been one of the biggest problems facing Ford and General Motors.

Both companies are trying to do something about configuration, but Ford is probably the more aggressive of the two. The company has begun to change its focus from producing whatever the factory could produce, and worrying later about selling it, to trying to closely match supply and demand. As part of this initiative, Ford is using configuration software to maintain rules about options and components, which will reduce the number of production mistakes and more closely match dealer orders to production schedules. Through a manufacturer/dealer partnership called FordDirect, Ford and its dealers also allow customers to browse dealer inventory, design a vehicle and match it to dealer inventory, and get a price quote and financing for a specific vehicle through the FordDirect.com Web site. FordDirect software is also used by dealers to track leads and measure the results from advertising. Ford has not yet entirely mastered the art of competing on configuration, but it is clearly making strides in that direction.

The industrial and farm equipment manufacturer Deere & Company is another firm that has invested heavily in analytics around configuration and product availability. On any particular Deere product line—say, for a tractor—there may be tens of thousands of valid configurations. Deere's goal was to reduce inventory and complexity by eliminating configurations that were least desirable to make and sell. Deere analysts worked with academics to find the optimal number of configurations on two product lines at Deere. Profits on the two lines were increased by 15 percent as a result of the analytical work, which allowed 30 to 50 percent reductions in the number of configurations offered to customers while maintaining high levels of customer service and satisfaction.[15]

For Internet-based businesses, *operations* means churning out the basic service for which customers visit a Web site. Successful online businesses use analytics to test virtually all aspects of their sites before implementing them broadly. At Google, for example, the primary reason customers visit the site is to use its search capabilities. Google has a very extensive program of testing and analytics with regard to its search engine. Google employs a wide range of operational and customer data and analytics to improve search attributes, including relevance, timeliness, and the user experience. The company developed many of its own proprietary measures of search relevance. Most of the metrics are gathered in an automated fashion, such as the percentage of foreign results, how deeply users go in the retrieved items list, the percentage of users who go to each page of the search result, and the measures of search latency or timeliness. But Google also collects human judgments on the search process, and even observes individual users (at Google headquarters and in users' homes) as they use the site for individual queries and entire sessions. One technique employed is eye tracking, from which "heat maps" are created showing which areas of a page receive the most attention.

Google is heavily committed to experimentation before making any change in its search site. As Bill Brougher, search product manager for Google, put it:

> Experiments are a requirement of launching a new feature. It's a very powerful tool for us. We have been experimenting for years and have accumulated a lot of institutional knowledge about what works. Before any new feature ships, it has to pass through a funnel involving several tests. For example, any change to our search algorithms has to be tested against our base-level search quality to make sure the change is a substantial improvement over the base. A little blip in quality isn't significant enough to adopt.[16]

Google's methods for analytical operations are as rigorous as any firm's, and the nature of the business makes a large amount of data available for analysis.

Research and Development Analytics

Research and development (R&D) has been perhaps the most analytical function within companies. It was the primary bastion of the scientific method within companies, featuring hypothesis testing, control groups, and statistical analysis.

Of course, some of this highly analytical work still goes on within R&D functions, although much of the basic research in R&D has been supplanted by applied research (which can still use analytical methods) and the creation of extensions of existing products. In several industries, research has become more mathematical and statistical in nature, as computational methods replace or augment traditional experimental approaches.

We'll describe the analytical environment for R&D in one industry that's changing dramatically with regard to analytics. In the pharmaceutical industry, analytics—particularly the analysis of clinical trials data to see whether drugs have a beneficial effect—always have been important. Over the last several years, however, there has been a marked growth in *systems biology*, in which firms attempt to integrate genomic, proteomic, metabolic, and clinical data from a variety of sources, create models and identify patterns in this data, correlate them to clinical outcomes, and eventually generate knowledge about diseases and their responses to drugs. This is a considerable challenge, however, and firms are just beginning to address it. We interviewed three pharmaceutical firms—one large "big pharma" company and two smaller, research-oriented firms—and found that all of them have efforts under way in this regard, but they are a long way from achieving the goal.

Analytics is also being used effectively to address today's challenges in R&D, and this is one way that Vertex Pharmaceuticals, Inc. competes.

Vertex, a global biotech firm headquartered in Cambridge, Mass., has taken a particularly analytical approach to R&D, and its results are beginning to show the payoff. Vertex's President and CEO, Joshua Boger, Ph.D. is a strong believer in the power of analytics to raise drug development productivity. As early as 1988 (when he left Merck & Co. to found Vertex) he argued that, *"What you need in this business is more information than the other guy. Not more smarts. Not more intuition. Just more information."*[17]

Vertex has undertaken a variety of analytical initiatives—in research, development, and marketing. In research, Vertex has focused on analyses that attempt to maximize the likelihood of a compound's success. This includes developing multiple patent lead series per project and ensuring that compounds have favorable drug-like attributes. Vertex's approach to drug design is known as rational or structural. This approach seeks to "design-in" drug-like properties from the beginning of a drug development project and it enables Vertex to determine as early as possible whether a compound will have drug-like attributes.

More of Vertex's efforts in using analytics have gone into the development stage of R&D, where its analyses indicate that most of the cost increases in the industry have taken place. One particularly high cost is the design of clinical trials. Poor clinical trial design leads to either ambiguous trial results or overly large clinical trials. This causes substantial delays and raises costs. Vertex has addressed this challenge by developing new trial simulation tools. These tools enable Vertex to design more informative and effective clinical trials in substantially less time. Vertex can now perform trial simulations hundreds of times faster than were previously possible. With these simulations, Vertex can also reduce the risk of failed or ambiguous trials caused by faulty trial design. This simulation advantage allows Vertex to optimize trial design in a fraction of the time it takes using industry standard design tools, thereby shortening the trial cycle time.

Clinical trial operation also represents some of the highest cost increases across the pharmaceutical industry. The operation of clinical trials, as with trial design, takes place within the development stage of R&D. Operational activities that are not automated lead to significant costs. Vertex uses analytics to automate and enhance clinical trial operations; examples include tools for patient accruals and electronic data capture (EDC).

Whether in R&D or elsewhere, the company begins with the right metric for the phenomenon it needs to optimize. Analysts determine how to obtain the appropriate data and what analyses to conduct. With these findings, Vertex constantly compares itself to competitors and to best practice benchmarks for the pharmaceutical industry. "We compete on analytics and culture," says Steve Schmidt, Vertex's chief information officer. "We encourage fearless pursuit of innovations but we ruthlessly measure the effect these innovations have on our core business. We're always looking for new meaningful analytic metrics, but where we look is driven by our strategy, our core corporate values and strengths, and our understanding of the value proposition to our business."[18] Vertex is a great example of applying analytics to product R&D, and as a result the company has an impressive array of new drugs in all stages of development.

The pharmaceutical industry is also pursuing analytical approaches that don't even involve the laboratory. So-called in silico research uses computational models of both patients and drugs to simulate experiments more rapidly and cheaply than they could be performed in a lab. One systems biology start-up, Entelos, Inc., has produced computer program "platforms" to simulate diseases and treatments in the areas of cardiovascular diseases, diabetes, inflammations, and asthma, among others. Entelos partners with pharmaceutical companies and other research organizations to identify and test new compounds. The goal is to use computational simulations to reduce the very high cost, long cycle times, and high failure rates of conventional laboratory research in the pharmaceutical industry. One collaboration on a diabetes drug between Entelos and Johnson & Johnson, for example, led to a 40 percent reduction in time and a 66 percent reduction in the number of patients necessary in an early-phase clinical trial.[19]

Of course, R&D today involves not only product innovation but also innovation in other domains: processes and operations; business models; customer innovations such as marketing, sales, and service; and new management approaches. In a very important sense, the idea behind this book is that each area in which an organization does business can be one in which R&D is conducted. In the previous chapter, we noted how Capital One identifies new offerings through its test-and-learn market research approach. At Internet-oriented firms such as Amazon.com, Yahoo!, and Google, every change to a Web page is treated as a small R&D project. What's the baseline case for measures such as page views, time spent on the site, and click-throughs? How does the change work on a small scale? How does it work when it is scaled more broadly? This test-and-learn approach to operational R&D is just as important as R&D on products.

Operational, business-model R&D also doesn't have to involve the Internet. Harvard professor Stefan Thomke has described, for example, the experimental approaches that Bank of America has adopted for customer service innovations in its retail branches.[20] Just as if it were developing new products in the laboratory, the bank treats each change in its service processes as an experiment and applies such approaches to experimental rigor as control groups, pilot studies, and statistical analysis.

In health care, research on service operations means finding better evidence-based medicine and treatment strategies for specific diseases. Despite the seemingly scientific nature of medicine, several studies suggest that only one-quarter to a third of medical decisions are based on science. A growing industry of health care providers, insurance companies, and third-party data and analytical service providers are working to make health care more efficient and effective through analytics.

One increasingly common approach, for example, is to try to predict the likelihood that members of a health plan will develop higher risk for more severe disease over time. Healthways is one company that works with insurers to make such predictions and to identify ways to improve health outcomes and thereby reduce the likely cost to the insurer. Healthways uses data on members' demographic, claims, prescription, and lab procedures to predict (using artificial intelligence neural network technology) which ones will be at highest risk for greater future total medical expenditures over the next year. Healthways employs more than fifteen-hundred registered nurses who then provide telephonic and direct mail interventions from one of its ten call centers nationwide to help members develop healthy behaviors which reduce the severity of the disease, improve outcomes, and reduce the cost to the health plan. This approach to risk management can also reduce ongoing health maintenance costs and lower the risk of disease recurrence.[21]

Other approaches to evidence-based health care involve developing appropriate treatment protocols for patients in health care facilities. Partners HealthCare in Boston, for example, has several initiatives under way to improve health care outcomes through protocols and "clinical decision support" for physicians and other care providers. Partners' first efforts were primarily around drug prescriptions because they are the least ambiguous approach to clinical care, but in several disease areas the organization has also developed a set of care protocols. Many of the clinical decision support "rules" are embedded in systems that are used when physicians input an order for a patient.[22] Other steps in evidence-based medicine for Partners include monitoring of patient data and events, making the right decisions the easiest decisions for caregivers, and predictive modeling of treatment and medical performance.

Human Resource Analytics

The final internal analytical application we'll discuss in this chapter is in human resources. As with other parts of organizations, the tools for employing analytics in HR are becoming widely available. Most large organizations now have in place human resource information systems (HRIS), which record basic HR transactions such as hiring date, compensation, promotions, and performance ratings. Some go well beyond that level, and record skill levels on a variety of aptitudes and learning programs undertaken to improve those skills. Companies increasingly have the ability to relate their investments in human capital to their returns on financial capital. Whether they have the desire, however, is another question. People may be "our most important asset," and even our most expensive asset, but they are rarely our most measured asset. Many companies may be beginning to employ HR analytics, but they are hardly competing on them.

The most conspicuous exception, of course, is in professional sports. Baseball, football, basketball, and soccer teams (at least outside the United States) pay high salaries to their players and have little other than those players to help them compete. Many successful teams are taking innovative approaches to the measurement of player abilities and the selection of players for teams. We've already talked about the analytical approach to player evaluation in baseball that was well described in Michael Lewis's *Moneyball*. In American professional football, the team that most exemplifies analytical HR is the New England Patriots, which has won three of the last five Super Bowls.

The Patriots take a decidedly different approach to HR than other teams in the National Football League (NFL). They don't use the same scouting services that other teams employ. They evaluate college players at the smallest, most obscure schools. They evaluate potential draft selections on the basis of criteria that other teams don't use—intelligence, for example, and a low level of egotism. As coach Bill Belichick puts it: "When you bring a player onto a team, you bring all that comes with him. You bring his attitude, his speed, strength, mental toughness, quickness. Our evaluation is comprehensive. Scott Pioli [vice president of player personnel] and the scouting department do a great job of getting a lot of details by going into the history of a player, his mental and physical makeup as well as attitude and character. He eventually receives one grade and that establishes his overall value to the team."[23]

Belichick often refers to the nonphysical attributes of players as "intangibles," and he is perfectly comfortable discussing them with players and media representatives.

The Patriots manage the potential player data in a Draft Decision Support System, which is updated daily with new reports from scouts. Cross-checkers at the team's offices check the scout ranking by comparing West Coast scout ratings with similar East Coast ratings (i.e., does the 6.2 UCLA player compare with the 6.2 Georgia Tech player?). No detail that can provide an edge is overlooked.

We don't know of any businesses that compete on HR analytics to this degree (other than perhaps Capital One, which we discuss later in the chapter), but the phenomenon is beginning to emerge. Companies are measuring more consistently across global HR processes and putting the information in systems. There are varying approaches to quantitative HR, including 360-degree evaluations, forced rankings, predictions about attrition, and so forth. None of these approach "rocket science," but they do connote a much more disciplined and methodical approach. At American Express, for example, which has employees in eighty-three countries, an HR executive in Asia commented, "Everything that we touch has a metric attached. Whatever we do we use globally consistent processes, measurements and databases. We do things in a methodical, thought out, consistent manner, and we have consistent platforms."[24]

Such global discipline is a prerequisite for serious HR analytics, and it's not hard to imagine that HR metrics will be used more for prediction and optimization in the future.

One organization taking HR analytics seriously is Sprint, the *Fortune* 50 wireless telecommunications company. The human resources team at Sprint discovered that employee relationships follow a predictable life cycle that is very similar to that of their customer relationships. Chad Jones, the vice president of customer management, worked with the HR team to translate Sprint's six-stage customer relationship life cycle into a series of similar stages and questions for HR, such as:

How do employees learn about Sprint?

How do we make sure we find and hire the most qualified candidates?

How are we going to get the employee up and running and get them productive?

How are we going to get them their first paycheck and make sure they are happy with that first paycheck?

How are we going to intervene when the employee is unhappy?

And how are we going to get the employee recommitted year after year to the business?

Sprint attempts to measure as many of these issues as possible for its employees and has found that the insights gained from this analysis help the company optimize each stage of its relationship with employees and promote a motivated, positive workforce.

The shift to "talent management" is also driving the move toward HR analytics. One manufacturing company we interviewed, for example, has developed a "talent management index" from four proprietary measures, and it uses the index to evaluate how each organizational unit manages its investments in human capital. Goldman Sachs, which, like professional sports teams, pays its employees extremely well, is beginning to apply analytical approaches to its workforce. General Electric, Accenture, and Procter & Gamble seek quantitative reasoning abilities in potential recruits. Harrah's, another analytical competitor in general, also uses HR analytics extensively in the recruiting process.

Another factor driving the shift to HR analytics is increasing rigor in staffing and recruiting processes. Companies are increasingly viewing these processes as activities that can be measured and improved; people are almost becoming just another supply chain resource. This is particularly noticeable in relationships with external staffing firms. Apex Systems, a fast-growing ($300 million in 2006 revenues) IT staffing firm based in Richmond, Virginia, has observed a long-term move among its clients to greater use of more rigorous processes and metrics in its clients, and it's trying to stay ahead of the trend by adopting more analytical measures and management approaches in its own business. Apex looks at a variety of staffing metrics, including the following:

- Time to respond with a first, second, and third qualified candidate

- How many candidates does a customer see

- Frequencies of payroll errors or customer invoice defects

- Speed of customer issue resolution

- Overall customer satisfaction levels

Apex's customers are increasingly using vendor management system (VMS) software to track the efficiency and effectiveness of staffing processes, so the company needs to establish and understand its own analytics to stay ahead of demand.

If there is any company that rivals the New England Patriots for HR analytics in the business world, it's Capital One. The company uses analytics extensively in the hiring process, requiring potential employees at all levels to take a variety of tests that measure their analytical abilities. The company uses mathematical case interviewing, a variety of behavioral and attitudinal tests, and multiple rounds of interviewing to ensure that it gets the people it wants. The process applies at all levels—even to the senior vice presidents who head business functions. For example:

> When Dennis Liberson flew into Washington to interview for the top human resources position at Capital One Financial Corp., he was told that his interviews with the 16 top executives would have to wait. First, he was whisked off to a hotel room to take an algebra exam and write a business plan. Liberson, who jokes nearly seven years later that he might have been "the only HR guy who could pass their math test," got the job and is now one of the company's executive vice presidents. He also got an early taste of Capital One's obsession with testing.[25]

Liberson is no longer the head of HR, but the focus on testing remains. A candidate for a managerial role at Capital One, for example, is still asked to review a set of financial statements and charts for a publishing company and then answer questions like these:

> What was the ratio of sales revenue to distribution costs for science books in 2002? (Round to nearest whole number):
>
> A. 27 to 1   B. 53 to 1   C. 39 to 1   D. 4 to 1   E. Cannot say

Even the most senior executive without some quantitative skills need not apply.

Overall, however, other than these few companies and professional sports teams, few organizations are truly competing on HR analytics. Perhaps this emphasis will come with time, but what seems to be lacking most is the management desire to compete on HR in the first place. Perhaps as people costs continue to rise and constitute higher percentages of organizations' total costs, and as executives realize that their people are truly their most critical resource, analytics will catch on and proliferate in HR.

This chapter has considered a wide variety of internal applications of analytics. In each case, our objective was to illustrate not just that analytics are possible in a particular function but that they can be the basis for a different approach to competition and strategy. We hope these examples will drive senior executives to think about their own strategies and how they perform their internal activities. The next chapter, which addresses the use of analytics in external (e.g., customer and supplier) relationships, offers even more possibilities for competition.

5

COMPETING ON ANALYTICS WITH EXTERNAL PROCESSES

Customer and Supplier Applications

ANALYTICS TOOK A GREAT LEAP forward when companies began using them to improve their external processes—those related to managing and responding to customer demand and supplier relationships. Once kept strictly segregated, the boundaries between customer relationship management (CRM) processes such as sales and marketing and supply chain management (SCM) processes such as procurement and logistics have been broken down by organizations seeking to align supply and demand more accurately. Unlike internal processes that lie completely within the organization's direct control, externally focused processes require cooperation from outsiders, as well as their resources. For those reasons, managing analytics related to external processes is a greater challenge.

Despite the challenge, many companies in a variety of industries are enhancing their CRM and SCM capabilities with predictive analytics, and they are enjoying market-leading growth and performance as a result.

Many companies generate descriptive statistics about external aspects of their business—average revenue per customer, for example, or average order size. But analytical competitors look beyond basic statistics and do the following:

- They use predictive modeling to identify the most profitable customers—as well as those with the greatest profit potential and the ones most likely to cancel their accounts.

- They integrate data generated in-house with data acquired from outside sources for a comprehensive understanding of their customers.

- They optimize their supply chains and can thus determine the impact of unexpected glitches, simulate alternatives, and route shipments around problems.

- They analyze historical sales and pricing trends to establish prices in real time and get the highest yield possible from each transaction.

- They use sophisticated experiments to measure the overall impact or "lift" of advertising and other marketing strategies and then apply their insights to future analyses.

Strange Bedfellows?

At first glance, supply chain management and customer relationship management would seem to have little in common. Supply chain management, on the one hand, seems like a natural fit for an analytical focus. For years, operations management specialists have created algorithms to help companies keep minimal levels of inventory on hand while preventing stock-outs—among other supply chain challenges. And manufacturing firms have long relied on sophisticated mathematical models to forecast demand, manage inventory, and optimize manufacturing processes. They also pursued quality-focused initiatives such as Six Sigma and *kaizen*, tools for which data analysis is an integral part of the methodology.

Customer relationship management, however, seems less amenable to analytical intervention—at least, that might be the common perception. The traditional focus in sales has been on the personal skills of salespeople—their ability to form long-term relationships and to put skeptical potential customers at ease. And marketing has long been viewed as a creative function whose challenge has been to understand customer behavior and convert that insight into inducements that will increase sales.

But the roots of analytics in business come from the customer side as much as the supplier side. Twenty years ago, consumer products firms like Procter & Gamble began using analytical software and databases to analyze sales and determine the parameters of product promotions. These companies invented the discipline of marketing-mix analytics to track the impact of individual investments such as trade promotions and coupon offers. They collected and analyzed data from vendors like ACNielsen and Information Resources, Inc. (IRI) to understand how their customers' (grocers) and consumers' behavior was influenced by different channels. These early innovators are being joined today by companies in virtually every industry, including retailers such as 7-Eleven Japan, manufacturers like Samsung, phone companies such as Verizon and Bouygues Telecom, and pharmaceutical companies such as AstraZeneca. More recently, marketing organizations have radically increased their analytical orientations with the rise of campaign management software. Quantitatively oriented marketers can now use these tools to experiment with different campaigns for different groups of customers and learn which campaigns work best for which audiences.

Analytical competitors, however, take the use of analytics much further than most companies. In many cases, they are pushing not only data but also the results of analyses to their customers. Our survey data suggests that they are also integrating their systems more thoroughly and sharing data with their suppliers.[1] As companies integrate data on products, customers, and prices, they find new opportunities that arise by aligning and integrating the activities of supply and demand. Instead of conducting post hoc analyses that allow them to correct future actions, they generate and analyze process data in near–real time and adjust their processes dynamically.

At Harrah's casinos, for example, customers use loyalty cards that capture data on their behavior. The data is used in near–real time by both marketing and operations to optimize yield, set prices for slots and hotel rooms, and design the optimal traffic flow through the casinos. Harrah's chief information officer, Tim Stanley, describes the change in orientation: "We are in a transition from analytical customer-relationship management, where customer data is analyzed and acted upon at a later time, to real-time customer analytics at the point of sale in the casino, where . . . action is taken on data as it is being collected."[2]

How does this work in practice? One example can be seen when a customer loses too much money too fast. Harrah's systems can identify this problem and almost immediately send a message (electronically or through a service representative) to the customer at a slot machine, such as, "Looks like you're having a tough day at the slots. It might be a good time to visit the buffet. Here's a $20 coupon you can use in the next hour." Harrah's is also experimenting with real-time marketing interventions over cell phones and PDAs that help customers manage their entire vacation experience in Las Vegas, where the company owns several adjacent properties. "There are two seats left for the Celine Dion concert tonight," a text message might say, "and we're making them available at half price because of your loyal play at Harrah's! Text 'yes, 2' if you'd like both tickets."

In the remainder of this chapter, we'll explain how other companies are taking advantage of their analytical abilities to optimize their customer and supplier processes.

Customer-Based Processes

Companies today face a critical need for robust customer-based processes. For one thing, acquiring and retaining customers is getting more expensive, especially in service-based industries such as telecommunications and financial services. And for another, consumers are harder to satisfy and more demanding.[3] To compete successfully in this environment, analytical competitors are pursuing a range of tactics that enable them to attract and retain customers more effectively, engage in "dynamic pricing," optimize their brand management, translate customer interactions into sales, manage customer life cycles, and differentiate their products by personalizing them (refer to "Typical Analytical Applications in Marketing" box on the next page).

Attracting and Retaining Customers

There are, of course, a variety of ways to attract and retain customers, and analytics can support most of them. One traditional means of attracting customers has been advertising. This industry has already been, and will continue to be, transformed by analytics. Two factors are most closely

Typical Analytical Applications in Marketing

CHAID. An abbreviation of *Chi-square automatic interaction detection*, this statistical technique is used to segment customers on the basis of multiple alternative variables. The analysis creates a segmentation "tree" and continues to add different variables, or branches, to the tree as long as it is statistically significant.

Conjoint analysis. Typically used to evaluate the strength and direction of customer preferences for a combination of product or service attributes. For example, a conjoint analysis might be used to determine which factors— price, quality, dealer location, and so on—are most important to customers who are purchasing a new car.

Lifetime value analysis. This analysis employs analytical models to assess the profitability of an individual customer (or a class of customers) over a lifetime of transactions. Sophisticated models generate accurate estimates of the costs incurred by the customer in buying and making use of the product, including the cost of the buying channel, the likelihood of returns, the expense from calls for customer service, and so on.

Market experiments. Using direct mail, changes in the Web site, promotions, and other techniques, marketers test variables to determine what customers respond to most in a given offering. Normally involves different treatments based on assumed causal variables for different (ideally randomized) groups, with an outcome measure and a comparison from which the effect of the treatment can be observed.

Multiple regression analysis. The most common statistical technique for predicting the value of a dependent variable (such as sales) in relation to one or more independent variables (such as the number of salespeople, the temperature, or the day of the month). While basic regression assumes linear relationships, modifications of the model can deal with nonlinearity, logarithmic relationships, and so forth.

Price optimization. Also known as yield or revenue management, this technique assumes that the primary causal variable in customer purchase behavior is price. The key issue is usually price elasticity, or the response (changes in demand) of the buyer to increases or decreases in product price. Price optimization initiatives typically construct price elasticity curves in order to understand the impact of price across a range of changes and conditions.

> **Time series experiments.** These experimental designs follow a particular population for successive points in time. They are used to determine whether a condition that applied at a certain point led to a change in the variables under study. This approach might be used, for example, to determine the impact of exposure to advertising on product purchases over time.

associated with the transformation. One is the econometric analysis of time series data to determine whether advertising is statistically associated with increased sales of a product or service. The other is the "addressable" and relatively easily analyzed nature of Web-based advertising, as exemplified by Google. We'll describe each of these briefly.

Econometric analysis has begun to address the age-old problem with advertising in traditional media, as described by department store pioneer John Wanamaker: "Half the money I spend on advertising is wasted; the trouble is, I don't know which half."

Sir Martin Sorrell, CEO of WPP Group, one of the world's largest advertising agencies, calls econometrics the holy grail of advertising. He noted in an interview, "There is no doubt in my mind that scientific analysis, including econometrics, is one of the most important areas in the marketing-services industry."[4]

Several advertising agencies have created groups of econometrics experts to do such analyses for clients. One example is DDB Matrix, which was spun out of the agency DDB in 1999. DDB Matrix gathers data for its clients, builds data warehouses, and analyzes the data to find answers to a variety of questions on advertising effectiveness. The questions include such issues as which medium is most effective, whether the additional cost of color is worthwhile in print advertising, and what days of the week are best to run ads. Obviously, a great deal of data must be gathered to rule out alternative explanations of advertising lift. CEO Doug Hughes describes the data for one client: "For example, with Dell we have, over the last seven years, built a warehouse with more than 1.5 million records containing data on all ads, print, radio, cable TV, etc. The application now has thousands of lines of custom code. This database started out quite small. We expect that firms will increasingly view analytics about advertising as a necessary adjunct to embarking upon any campaign. Otherwise, advertising resources can hardly be considered well spent."[5]

The other dramatic change in advertising is the rise of online, Web-based ads. These are revolutionary, of course, because whether someone clicks on an ad can be tracked. There are a variety of Web-based advertising approaches—banners, pop-ups, search-based, and more—and the effectiveness of each can be easily tracked. One of the most powerful forms of online advertising is the search-based ad exemplified by Google. By having the industry-leading search engine, Google can serve ads that correspond to search terms (AdWords) used by a potential customer. Google also serves ads onto other companies' online properties through its AdSense network. The popularity of search-based advertising has fueled Google's rapid growth in revenues and profits.

One of the reasons Google has been successful with advertisers is its extensive use of analytics. Because Google advertising is done for a large client base for small payment increments (a few cents per click-through), much of the analytics must be automated and highly scalable. Google employs self-learning algorithms that are constantly analyzing the efficacy (typically in conversion rates) of different keywords (the primary advertising medium on Google's own properties), placement on the page, creative material, and so forth. The learning is input for an optimization engine that develops suggestions for advertisers without any human intervention. Advertisers can see the suggestions when they look at the reports for activity relative to their ads. The suggestions may differ for different types of sites, such as entertainment versus publishing. Large Google advertisers also have account managers who can work with the advertiser and provide analytics-based advice. Google's philosophy is that analytics and metrics will make advertisers more successful in working with the company, so they try to provide as much analytical sophistication as advertisers can use. Thus far the analytically intensive approach seems to have paid off in advertiser loyalty and Google's growth.

Other approaches to customer analytics primarily focus on retention and cross-selling. For example, the Norwegian bank DnB NOR has built analytics on top of a Teradata warehouse to more effectively build customer relationships. The bank uses "event triggers" in the data warehouse to prompt customer relationship analysts to offer one or more tailored services based on the event. For example, if a customer receives a substantial inheritance, a bank representative will call on the customer to offer investment products. DnB NOR has a set of automated tools that match customer profiles and events and then generate a set of suggested products. Based on customers' past experience, DnB then chooses the most effective channel through which to contact a customer about the most appropriate products. Using these tools, the company has achieved a conversion rate on cross-selling between 40 and 50 percent and has halved its marketing budget while increasing customer satisfaction.[6]

One of the most impressive users of analytics to retain customers is Tesco. Founded in 1924, Tesco is now the largest food retailer in the United Kingdom and one of the world's largest retailers. Located in thirteen countries, it operates in every form of retail food channel—convenience, specialty, supermarket, and hypermarket. Tesco's spectacular transformation began in 1995, when it introduced its loyalty card, the Clubcard. The card functions as a mechanism for collecting information on customers, rewarding customers for shopping at Tesco, and targeting coupon variations for maximum return. Customers earn points that are redeemable at Tesco at a rate of 1 percent of purchase amounts. Tesco estimates it has awarded points worth £1 billon.

The results are impressive. While the direct marketing industry's average response is only 2 percent, Tesco's coupon redemption rate is 20 percent and ranges as high as 50 percent. The company's CEO, Sir Terry Leahy, believes the Clubcard program is also responsible for the company's success with its Internet business. The world's largest Internet grocer, Tesco has delivered food to more than a million homes and serves four hundred thousand repeat customers. All online Tesco customers must have a Clubcard, so Tesco can know what they purchase and target online promotions accordingly. By analyzing Clubcard data, combined with a rigorous program of experimentation, Tesco's Internet business has seen sales surge for nonfood items including home furnishings, music downloads, and homeowner and automobile insurance.

Tesco uses the data it collects on purchases to group customers according to lifestyle. For example, a female shopper who makes weekly purchases, buys what's on sale, and uses coupons sent in the mail is considered a value-conscious customer. A male shopper who makes three to four purchases per week, all for prepared meals, and rarely changes his purchases regardless of price promotions is considered a convenience-conscious customer. With this kind of insight into its customers, Tesco then tailors its promotions to its customers' priorities and interests. Tesco says that it issues 7 million targeted variations of product coupons a year, driving the coupon redemption rate, customer loyalty, and ultimately financial performance to market-leading heights.[7]

Firms also use analytics to avoid bad customers while attracting the few customers who defy conventional measures of suitability or risk—an approach known as *skimming the cream off the garbage*. As we mentioned in chapter 3, Progressive Insurance and Capital One both eschew the traditional industry-standard risk measures. At Progressive, for example, instead of automatically rating a motorcycle rider as a high risk, analysts take into account such factors as the driver's employment history, participation in other high-risk activities (such as skydiving), and credit score. A driver with a long record with one employer who is also a low credit risk and avoids other risky activities will be rated as a low-risk customer.

Capital One has improved upon conventional approaches to attracting so-called subprime customers—those individuals who by their credit rating are considered to be a high risk for bankruptcy or default. Capital One employs its own proprietary consumer creditworthiness assessment tool to identify and attract those customers it sees as less risky than their credit scores would indicate.

Pricing Optimization

Pricing is another task that is particularly susceptible to analytical manipulation. Companies use analytics for a competitive advantage by pricing products appropriately, whether that is Wal-Mart's everyday low pricing or a hotelier's adjusting prices in response to customer demand. Analytics also make it easier to engage in *dynamic pricing*—the practice of adjusting the price for a good or service in real time in response to market conditions such as demand, inventory level, competitor behavior, and customer history. This tactic was pioneered in the airline industry but now has spread to other sectors.

Retail prices, for example, have historically been set by intuition. Today, however, many retailers are adopting analytical software as part of "scientific retailing." Such software works by analyzing a retailer's historical point-of-sale data to determine price elasticity and cross-elasticity (a measure of whether one good is a substitute for another) for every item in every store. An equation is calculated that determines the optimal price to maximize sales and profitability.

Retailers usually begin by using pricing analytics to optimize mark-downs—figuring out when and by how much to lower prices. Some then move on to pricing for all retail merchandise and to analysis of pro-motions, category mix, and breadth and depth of assortments. Most re-tailers experience a 5 percent to 10 percent increase in gross margin as a result of using price optimization systems. Some yield even greater benefits. According to a Yankee Group report, "Enterprises have real-ized up to 20% profit improvements by using price management and profit optimization (PMPO) solutions. No other packaged software can deliver the same type of top-line benefits and address bottom-line inef-ficiencies. PMPO is the best kept secret in enterprise software."[8]

JCPenney was one of the earliest large retailers to adopt price opti-mization software and processes. A few years ago, the company began an analytically intensive program that integrated merchandising, pric-ing optimization, and the supply chain. This approach helped the com-pany add five points of gross margin, increase inventory turns by 10 percent, and grow top-line and comparative store sales for four consec-utive years (2001 through 2004). Operating profits also grew at double-digit rates.[9]

Analytically based pricing software is spreading to other industries as well. In fact, 77 percent of the large business-to-business U.S. enter-prise respondents to a 2006 Yankee Group survey that are not already using price management software reported that they have developed a business case to purchase that software.[10]

When combined with other analytic data, dynamic pricing can pro-vide a strategic advantage in the face of changing market conditions. At Dell, the chief financial officer used the company's forecasting system to anticipate the economic downturn of 2000 and 2001. While com-petitors like Hewlett-Packard and Compaq remained optimistic, Dell cut costs and slashed prices. Dell was able to weather the recession with only a slight downturn in sales—2.3 percent in 2001. Compared with Hewlett-Packard (sales down by 32 percent), Compaq (down 36 per-cent), and Gateway (down 62 percent), Dell was a success, and its in-creased market share poised the company for greater success when the economy rebounded.

One cautionary note: most consumers are used to the idea of dynamic pricing in the context of changing market conditions—resorts that lower room prices during the off-season and raise them during peak demand, for example—and probably find it fair. However, companies can face a backlash when they use demand elasticity (the fact that loyal customers will pay a higher price for something than fickle customers) to make pricing decisions. For example, for a time, Amazon.com priced its DVDs higher to people who spent more. When that practice became known to the public, Amazon.com was forced to retreat by the resulting outcry.

Brand Management

Just as analytics bring a heightened level of discipline to pricing, they also bring needed discipline to marketing activities as a whole. Leading companies have developed analytical capabilities that enable them to efficiently design and execute highly effective multichannel marketing campaigns, measure the results, and continually improve future campaigns. Many are using econometric modeling and scenario planning to predict performance outcomes depending on overall budget levels or how much is spent in different channels.

Consider the challenge faced by Samsung in 1999. At the time, the company sold 14 product categories in more than 200 countries in a total of 476 category–country combinations. Amid that complexity, the company struggled to allocate marketing resources effectively. It collected data sporadically and unsystematically and analyzed it only at the country level. Further, its definitions of data, collection procedures, and reporting conventions were not standardized, so interregional analysis was impractical, if not impossible.

This was the situation awaiting Eric Kim when he joined Samsung in 1999 as executive vice president of global marketing. With a worldwide marketing budget of $1 billion, Kim launched an eighteen-month project to gather detailed information on those 476 combinations; assemble and integrate country-level data on a single, easy-to-use site accessible from Samsung marketers' desktops; use brand data to better set marketing objectives by country and product; and employ the analytical power of software to predict the impact of different resource allocations.

The project resulted in the development of a system called M-Net that not only houses reams of data but also provides the analytic tools needed to make sense of it. Now Samsung managers can assess primary marketing objectives, analyze the results of recent marketing investments around the globe, and build predictive models and what-if scenarios to test future investments. Among other things, M-Net has saved the company millions of dollars by revealing mismatches between some of the company's marketing investments and the maximum returns those investments could ever yield. Today Samsung allocates marketing resources after systematic analysis of product or geographic market potential, not historical performance.[11]

In Samsung's case, analytics were required to maximize the company's return on its marketing investment. In other cases, industry limitations require creative solutions to acquire the data needed to stay ahead of competitors. Beer, wine, and spirits producers, for example, compete in an industry that is highly dependent on in-store promotions to boost sales, increase market share, and defend against competitors' encroachments. Each company has access to some sales data from its distributors and external information providers, such as Information Resources, Inc. But these companies have little visibility into the hundreds of thousands of retailers that sell their products to consumers.

Anheuser-Busch Companies successfully surmounted this obstacle through the creative use of mobile technology and an analytical system called BudNet. The brewer derives financial benefits from BudNet by using this information to optimize product mix and price at the local retailer level. The company also uses information from the system to develop local marketing and advertising strategies that are unique to the market.

How does BudNet work in practice? Anheuser-Busch guards details about the system carefully and treats it as a mission-critical weapon. In brief, however, the company arms both company-owned and independent distributors with data entry devices. The devices allow the reps to update inventory levels, but they are also used for a more strategic objective. A sales rep will walk around retail stores looking at the shelf space, displays, and inventory levels of Anheuser-Busch products, as well as the displays, pricing, and shelf space of competitor products. The rep uses a cell phone to upload this data.

Through BudNet, data from thousands of distributor sales reps gives Anheuser-Busch unparalleled insight into what happens to its products at the retail level. The company knows whether a six-pack of Bud Light was warm or cold, whether it was on sale, and what the price of Bud Light was at other stores in the area. In combination with data from IRI (which supplies data on all scanned alcoholic beverages), the BudNet data helps Anheuser-Busch offer even more effective marketing. The company knows that St. Patrick's Day promotions work poorly in Atlanta, for example, but well in St. Louis. The result has been consistent growth for Anheuser-Busch while major competitors like Coors Brewing Company and Miller Brewing Company have experienced flat or declining sales.[12] Other beverage manufacturers have taken notice of BudNet's impact and have begun to imitate its analytical capability. Gallo, for example, has a program called the Gallo Edge that allows its retailers to optimize the profitability of the shelf space devoted to wine products.

Converting Customer Interactions into Sales

The strategies described so far relate to arm's-length interactions between companies and customers, but it is also possible to use analytics to improve the face-to-face encounters between customers and salespeople. Consider how Capital One Health Care, which sells financing services through medical practices for uninsured medical procedures (like cosmetic surgery), outsmarts competitors. Most financing firms market their credit services to doctors the same way many pharmaceutical reps do—known in the business as "pens, pads, and pizza." By stopping by at lunchtime, representatives hope they can entice the doctor out for a quick lunch break and an even shorter sales pitch. At Capital One, however, reps don't randomly chase down prospects and hope that a few freebies will clinch the deal. Instead, analysts supply the company's reps with information about which doctors to target and which sales messages and products are most likely to be effective.

Best Buy is another company that is acting on knowledge gained through customer interactions to improve those interactions (and, not incidentally, to boost sales). Over the last five years, the company has collected data on 60 million U.S. households. To maximize financial performance in each retail store, Best Buy used data-driven insights to develop profiles of eight customer segments.

To translate their insights into increased sales and market share, however, Best Buy needed to understand the best way to serve each segment. It began by establishing a few stores as laboratories. CEO Brad Anderson describes these stores as "our R&D arm for researching customer segments and the value propositions that matter to them."[13] The company used analytics to determine, for example, the impact of pricing changes not only on short-term sales velocity but also on the overall customer experience and its long-term impact on customer perception and sales. It even studied the behavior in each segment of *frequent returners*—people who commonly seek to exchange products or return them as defective—to learn how to better satisfy these customers.

Incorporating the insights from data analysis and testing at the lab stores, Best Buy developed new store formats for each segment. A "Barry" store, for example, is targeted to young, male audiophiles and videophiles and contains a home theater store-within-a-store. "Jill" stores are oriented to practical, short-on-time mothers. In this format, personal shoppers are available since they are both useful to "Jill" and are a feature that dramatically increases average spending per customer. Other changes are more subtle; for example, the volume on background music is lower than it is in other formats.

As stores convert to these formats, employees are educated about the customer segments who shop at their stores and the best way to serve them. Anderson sees the changes to employee behavior as critical: "We encourage employees to ask customers lifestyle questions and engage in fresh dialogue so that they can recommend suitable solutions. Then we train employees to hypothesize, test, and verify new ways to meet specific needs of the local population."[14]

Best Buy also trains employees to understand financial metrics, such as return on invested capital, so that they can gauge for themselves the effectiveness of customized merchandising displays. Specialized salespeople, such as home theater experts, get additional training that may last weeks. While exact figures are not available, "customer-centricity" based on analytics has delivered significant business results to Best Buy—the new stores formatted around specific customer segments are generating sales at twice the rate of Best Buy's traditional format.[15]

Harrah's is also able to use the information it collects to improve the experience of the customer while simultaneously streamlining casino traffic. Customers hate to wait; they may be tempted to leave. Worse, from the casino's perspective, a waiting customer is not spending money. When bottlenecks occur at certain slot machines, the company can offer a customer a free game at a slot machine located in a slower part of the casino. It can also inform waiting customers of an opening at another machine. These prompts help redirect traffic and even out demand. According to Wharton School professor David Bell, Harrah's is able to tell "who is coming into the casino, where they are going once they are inside, how long they sit at different gambling tables and so forth. This allows them to optimize the range, and configuration, of their gambling games."[16]

Managing Customer Life Cycles

In addition to facilitating the purchases of a customer on a given day, companies want to optimize their customers' lifetime value. Predictive analytics tools help organizations understand the life cycle of individual customer purchases and behavior. Best Buy's predictive models enable the company to increase subsequent sales after an initial purchase. Someone who buys a digital camera, for example, will receive a carefully timed e-coupon from Best Buy for a photo printer.

Sprint also takes a keen interest in customer life cycles. It uses analytics to address forty-two attributes that characterize the interactions, perceptions, and emotions of customers across a six-stage life cycle, from initial product awareness through service renewal or upgrade. The company integrates these life cycle analytics into its operations, using twenty-five models to determine the best ways to maximize customer loyalty and spending over time.

Sprint's goal is to have every customer "touch point" make the "next best offer" to the customer while eliminating interactions that might be perceived as nuisances. When Sprint discovered, for example, that a significant percentage of customers with unpaid bills were not deadbeats but individuals and companies with unresolved questions about their accounts, it shifted these collections from bill collectors to *retention agents*, whose role is to resolve conflicts and retain satisfied customers.

According to Sprint, the group responsible for these analytics has delivered more than $1 billion of enterprise value and $500 million in revenue by reducing customer churn, getting customers to buy more, and improving satisfaction rates.

Personalizing Content

A final strategy for using analytics to win over customers is to tailor offerings to individual preferences.

In the mobile network business, companies are vying to boost average revenue per user by selling subscribers information (such as news alerts and stock updates) and entertainment services (such as music downloads, ringtones, and video clips). But given the small screen on mobile devices, navigating content is a real challenge.

O2, a mobile network operator in the United Kingdom, uses analytics to help mobile users resolve that challenge. The company pioneered the use of artificial intelligence software to provide subscribers with the content they want before they know they want it. Analytical technology monitors subscriber behavior, such as the frequency with which users click on specific content, to determine personal preferences. The software then places desirable content where users can get to it easily.

The vast majority (97 percent) of O2's subscribers have opted to use personalized menus and enjoy the convenience of having a service that can predict and present content to match their tastes. Today, O2 has more than 50 percent of mobile Internet traffic in the United Kingdom, and the company continues to explore new ways to use analytics; for instance, it is investigating new collaborative filtering technology that would analyze the preferences of similar customers to make content suggestions. Hugh Griffiths, O2's head of data products, believes that "personalization is our key service differentiator."[17]

Supplier-Facing Processes

Contemporary supply chain processes blur the line between customer- and supplier-oriented processes. In some cases, customers penetrate deep into and across an organization, reaching all the way to suppliers. In other cases, companies are managing logistics for their customers (refer to "Typical Analytical Applications in Supply Chains" box on the next page).

Connecting Customers and Suppliers

The mother of all supply chain analytics competitors is Wal-Mart. The company collects massive amounts of sales and inventory data (583 terabytes as of April 2006) into a single integrated technology platform. Its managers routinely analyze manifold aspects of its supply chain, and store managers use analytical tools to optimize product assortment; they examine not only detailed sales data but also qualitative factors such as the opportunity to tailor assortments to local community needs.[18]

The most distinctive element of Wal-Mart's supply chain data is its availability to suppliers. Wal-Mart buys products from more than 17,400 suppliers in eighty countries, and each one uses the company's Retail Link system to track the movement of its products—in fact, the system's use is mandatory. In aggregate, suppliers run 21 million queries on the data warehouse every year, covering such data as daily

Typical Analytical Applications in Supply Chains

Capacity planning. Finding the capacity of a supply chain or its elements; identifying and eliminating bottlenecks; typically employs iterative analysis of alternative plans.

Demand–supply matching. Determining the intersections of demand and supply curves to optimize inventory and minimize overstocks and stock-outs. Typically involves such issues as arrival processes, waiting times, and throughput losses.

Location analysis. Optimization of locations for stores, distribution centers, manufacturing plants, and so on. Increasingly uses geographic analysis and digital maps to, for example, relate company locations to customer locations.

Modeling. Creating models to simulate, explore contingencies, and optimize supply chains. Many of these approaches employ some form of linear programming software and solvers, which allow programs to seek particular goals, given a set of variables and constraints.

Routing. Finding the best path for a delivery vehicle around a set of locations. Many of these approaches are versions of the "traveling salesman problem."

Scheduling. Creating detailed schedules for the flow of resources and work through a process. Some scheduling models are "finite" in that they take factory capacity limits into account when scheduling orders. So-called advanced planning and scheduling approaches also recognize material constraints in terms of current inventory and planned deliveries or allocations.

sales, shipments, purchase orders, invoices, claims, returns, forecasts, radio frequency ID deployments, and more.[19] Suppliers also have access to the Modular Category Assortment Planning System, which they can use to create store-specific modular layouts of products. The layouts are based on sales data, store traits, and data on ten consumer segments. Some suppliers have created more than one thousand modular layouts.

As Wal-Mart's data warehouse introduced additional information about customer behavior, applications using Wal-Mart's massive database began to extend well beyond their supply chain. Wal-Mart now collects more data about more consumers than anyone in the private sector. Wal-Mart marketers mine this data to ensure that customers have the products they want, when they want them, and at the right price. For example, they've learned that before a hurricane, consumers stock up on food items that don't require cooking or refrigeration. The top seller: Strawberry Pop Tarts. We expect that Wal-Mart asks Kellogg to rush shipments of them to stores just before a hurricane hits. In short, there are many analytical applications behind Wal-Mart's success as the world's largest retailer.

Wal-Mart may be the world's largest retailer, but at least it knows where all its stores are located. Amazon.com's business model, in contrast, requires the company to manage a constant flow of new products, suppliers, customers, and promotions, as well as deliver orders directly to its customers by promised dates. With one of the most complex supply chain problems in business, Amazon.com recruited Gang Yu, a professor of management science and a software entrepreneur who is one of the world's leading authorities on optimization analytics, as the head of its global supply chain.

Yu and his team began by integrating all the elements of their supply chain in order to coordinate supplier sourcing decisions. To determine the optimal sourcing strategy (determining the right mix of joint replenishment, coordinated replenishment, and single sourcing) as well as manage all the logistics to get a product from manufacturer to customer, Amazon.com applies advanced optimization and supply chain management methodologies and techniques across its fulfillment, capacity expansion, inventory management, procurement, and logistics functions.

For example, after experimenting with a variety of packaged software solutions and techniques, Yu concluded that no existing approach to modeling and managing supply chains would fit their needs. They ultimately invented a proprietary inventory model employing nonstationary stochastic optimization techniques, which allows them to model and optimize the many variables associated with their highly dynamic, fast-growing business.

Amazon.com sells over thirty categories of goods, from books to groceries to industrial and scientific tools. The company has a variety of fulfillment centers for different goods. When Amazon.com launches a new goods category, it uses analytics to plan the supply chain for the goods and leverage the company's existing systems and processes. To do so, it forecasts demand and capacity at the national level and fulfill-ment center level for each SKU. Its supply chain analysts try to optimize order quantities to satisfy constraints and minimize holding, shipping, and stock-out costs. In order to optimize its consumer goods supply chain, for example, it used an "integral min-cost flow problem with side constraints"; to round off fractional shipments, it used a "multiple knapsack problem using the greedy algorithm."

Logistics Management

Sometimes a service company uses analytics with such skill and execu-tion that entire lines of business can be created. United Parcel Service (UPS) took this route in 1986, when it formed UPS Logistics, a wholly owned subsidiary of UPS Supply Chain Solutions. UPS Logistics pro-vides routing, scheduling, and dispatching systems for businesses with private fleets and wholesale distribution.[20] The company claims to have over one thousand clients that use its services daily. This approach, cap-tured in the "Don't You Worry about a Thing" campaign, is enabling UPS to expand its reputation from reliable shipping to reliable handling of clients' logistics value chains.

Of course, UPS has been an analytical competitor in supply chains for many years. In 1954 its CEO noted, "Without operations research we'd be analyzing our problems intuitively only."[21] The company has long been known in its industry for truck route optimization and, more recently, airplane route optimization. The current UPS CEO, Mike Eskew, founded UPS's current operations research group in 1987. By 2003 he announced that he expected savings from optimization of $600 million annually. He described the importance of route optimiza-tion: "It's vital that we manage our networks around the world the best way that we can. When things don't go exactly the way we expected be-cause volume changes or weather gets in the way, we have to think of the best ways to recover and still keep our service levels."[22]

FedEx has also embraced both analytics and the move to providing full logistics outsourcing services to companies. While UPS and FedEx both provide customers with a full range of IT-based analytical tools, FedEx provides these applications to firms that do not engage its full lo-gistics services, leading one analyst to observe, "FedEx is as much a technology company as a shipping company."[23] UPS and FedEx have become so efficient and effective in all aspects of the logistics of ship-ping that other companies have found it to their economic advantage to outsource their entire logistics operations.

Another company helping its customers manage logistics is CEMEX, the leading global supplier of cement. Cement is highly per-ishable; it begins to set as soon as a truck is loaded, and the producer has limited time to get it to its destination. In Mexico, traffic, weather, and an unpredictable labor market make it incredibly hard to plan deliveries accurately. So a contractor might have concrete ready for delivery when the site isn't ready, or work crews might be at a standstill because the concrete hasn't arrived.

CEMEX realized that it could increase market share and charge a premium to time-conscious contractors by reducing delivery time on orders. To figure out how to accomplish that goal, CEMEX staffers stud-ied FedEx, pizza delivery companies, and ambulance squads. Following this research, CEMEX equipped most of its concrete-mixing trucks in Mexico with global positioning satellite locators and used predictive an-alytics to improve its delivery processes. This approach allows dispatch-ers to cut the average response time for changed orders from three hours to twenty minutes.[24] Not only did this system increase truck pro-ductivity by 35 percent, it also wedded customers firmly to the brand.[25]

CEMEX's strategy was powerful because the company changed its focus from the sale of a commodity to the sale of something customers really cared about. In short, the unit of business shifted from cubic yards to the delivery window. This was a simple change in one sense. But CEMEX then oriented its information, logistics, and delivery infra-structure around the delivery window concept, creating far-reaching changes in the company and eventually throughout the industry.[26]

Conclusion

Analytical competitors have recognized that the lines between supply and demand have blurred. As a result, they are using sophisticated ana-lytics in their supply chain and customer-facing processes to create dis-tinctive capabilities that help them serve their customers better and work with their suppliers more effectively.

The discipline of supply chain management has deep roots in ana-lytical mastery; companies that have excelled in this area have a decades-long history of using quantitative analysis to optimize logistics. Companies getting a later start, however, have clear opportunities to embrace an analytical approach to customer relationship management and other demand processes.

In part I of this book, we have described the nature of analytical competition. In part II, we lay out the steps companies need to take and the key technical and human resources needed for analytical competition.

Part Two

Building an Analytical
Capability

6

A Road Map to Enhanced Analytical Capabilities

Progressing Through the Five Stages of Development

By this point, developing an analytical capability may seem straightforward. Indeed, some organizations such as Marriott and Procter & Gamble have been using intensive data analysis for decades. Others, such as Google, Amazon.com, Netflix, and Capital One, were founded with the idea of using analytics as the basis of competition. These firms, with their history of close attention to data, sponsorship from senior management, and enterprise use of analytics, have attained the highest stage of analytical capability.

The overwhelming majority of organizations, however, have neither a finely honed analytical capability nor a detailed plan to develop one. For companies that want to become analytical competitors, a quick and painless journey cannot be promised. There are many moving pieces to put in place, including software applications, technology, data, processes, metrics, incentives, skills, culture, and sponsorship. One executive we interviewed compared the complexity of managing the development of analytical capabilities to playing a fifteen-level chess game.

Once the pieces fall into place, it still takes time for an organization to get the large-scale results it needs to become an analytical competitor. Changing business processes and employee behaviors is always the most difficult and time-consuming part of any major organizational change. And by its nature, developing an analytical capability is an iterative process, as managers gain better insights into the dynamics of their business over time by working with data and refining analytical models. Our research and experience suggests that it takes eighteen to thirty-six months of regularly working with data to start developing a steady stream of rich insights that can be translated into practice. Many organizations, lacking the will or faced with other pressing priorities, will take much longer than that.

Even highly analytical companies have lots of work left to do to improve their analytical capabilities. For example, Sprint, which used analytics to realize more than $1 billion of value and $500 million in incremental revenue over five years, believes that it has just scratched the surface of what it can accomplish with its analytical capability. And managers at a bank that has been an analytical competitor for years reported that different units are slipping back into silos of disaggregated customer data. Analytical competitors cannot rest on their laurels.

Nevertheless, the benefits of becoming an analytical competitor far outweigh the costs. In this chapter, we will introduce a road map that describes how organizations become analytical competitors and the benefits associated with each stage of the development process.

Overview of the Road Map

The road map describes typical behaviors, capabilities, and challenges at each stage of development. It provides guidance on investments and actions that are necessary to build an organization's analytical capabilities and move to higher stages of analytical competition.

Figure 6-1 provides an overview of the road map to analytical competition and the exit criteria for each stage.

Stage 1: Prerequisites to Analytical Competition

At stage 1, organizations lack the prerequisites for analytics. These companies need first to improve their transaction data environment in order to have consistent, quality data for decision making. If a company has poor-quality data, it should postpone plans for analytical competition and fix its data first. Dow Chemical's path is instructive. It began in-

FIGURE 6-1

Road map to becoming an analytical competitor

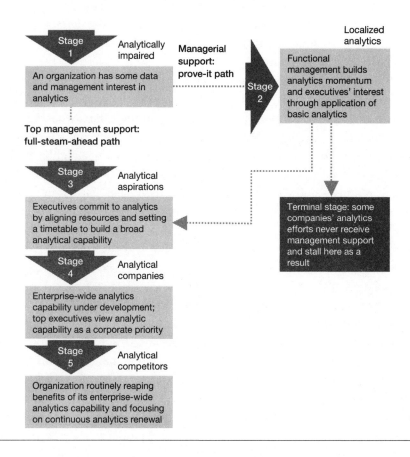

stalling one of the first SAP systems in the United States in the late 1980s but did not begin serious initiatives to use data analytically until enough transaction data had been accumulated.

Even if an organization has some quality data available, it must also have executives who are predisposed to fact-based decision making. A "data-allergic" management team that prides itself on making gut-based decisions is unlikely to be supportive. Any analytical initiatives in such an organization will be tactical and limited in impact.

Once a company has surmounted these obstacles, it is ready to advance to a critical juncture in the road map.

Assessing Analytical Capabilities

Once an organization has some useful data and management support in place, the next task is to take stock and candidly assess whether it has the strategic insight, sponsorship, culture, skills, data, and IT needed for analytical competition.

Barbara Desoer, Bank of America's global technology, service, and fulfillment executive, offers sage advice to anyone getting started: "Begin with an assessment—how differentiated is your offering versus what you and your customers want it to be? If it needs to be more, then you've got to find ways to create more value that comes from the knowledge you have. You have to come to that realization first; otherwise, don't bother with building data warehouses and CRM systems. You have to have that vision of what value looks like if you are going to figure out how to unleash that vision."[1]

While each stage of the road map reflects the ability of an enterprise to compete on analytics, different parts of the organization may be in very different stages of development. For example, actuarial work requires an appreciation of statistical methods that may not exist to the same extent in other parts of an insurance company. Or a pharmaceutical firm's marketing analytics in the United States may be far more sophisticated than they are in other countries or regions simply because the U.S. operation has greater access to data and an analytically minded manager in charge.

Just as some business units or processes may be more or less advanced than others in the enterprise, some aspects of the business are likely to be more analytically astute than others. For example, an organization may have a tightly integrated, highly standardized, and flexible IT environment but little demand for analytics, or, conversely, the demand for analytics far outstrips the capabilities of the IT organization. There may be many user departments and even individuals with their own analytical applications and data sources but little central coordination or synergy.

Organizations need to assess their level of analytical capability in three areas. (Table 6-1 provides an overview of the key attributes, each of which is equally vital to successful analytical competition.) One cautionary note: executives are often tempted to just obtain the data and analytical software they need, thinking that analytics are synonymous with technology. But unless executives consciously address the other elements, they will find it difficult to progress to later stages.

TABLE 6-1

The key elements in an analytical capability

Capabilities	Key elements
Organization	• Insight into performance drivers • Choosing a distinctive capability • Performance management and strategy execution • Process redesign and integration
Human	• Leadership and senior executive commitment • Establishing a fact-based culture • Securing and building skills • Managing analytical people
Technology	• Quality data • Analytic technologies

We'll address the organizational issues in this chapter and go into greater detail on the human factors in chapter 7 and the technical ones in chapter 8.

A company needs a clear strategy in order to know which data to focus on, how to allocate analytical resources, and what it is trying to accomplish. For example, the business strategy at Harrah's Entertainment dictated the company's analytical strategy as well. When the explosion of newly legalized gaming jurisdictions in the mid-1990s ground to a halt, Harrah's managers realized that growth could no longer come from the construction of new casinos. They knew that growth would need to come from existing casinos and from an increase of customer visits across Harrah's multiple properties. To achieve this goal, the company set a new strategic focus to drive growth through customer loyalty and data-driven marketing operations. This strategic focus enables Harrah's to concentrate its investments on the activities and processes that have the greatest impact on financial performance—its distinctive capability. Implementing this strategy required the company to expand and exploit the data it had amassed on the gaming behaviors and resort preferences of existing customers. (See the box "Choosing a Strategic Focus" for examples of where companies chose to focus their initial analytical investments.)

Choosing a Strategic Focus

Organizations initially focus on one or two areas for analytical competition:

- Harrah's: Loyalty plus service

- New England Patriots: Player selection plus fan experience

- Dreyfus Corporation: Equity analysis plus asset attrition

- UPS: Operations plus customer data

- Wal-Mart: Supply chain plus marketing

- Owens & Minor: Internal logistics plus customer cost reduction

- Progressive: Pricing plus new analytical service offerings

To have a significant impact on business performance, analytical competitors must continually strive to quantify and improve their insights into their performance drivers—the causal factors that drive costs, profitability, growth, and shareholder value in their industry (only the most advanced organizations have attempted to develop an enterprise-wide model of value creation). In practice, most organizations build their understanding gradually over time in a few key areas, learning from each new analysis and experiment.

To decide where to focus their resources for the greatest strategic impact, managers should answer the following questions:

- How can we distinguish ourselves in the marketplace?

- What is our distinctive capability?

- What key decisions in those processes, and elsewhere, need support from analytical insights?

- What information really matters to the business?

- What are the information and knowledge leverage points of the firm's performance?

As organizations develop greater insights, they can incorporate them into analytical models and adapt business processes to leverage them and increase competitive differentiation. These strategically focused insights, processes, and capabilities form the basis of the organization's distinctive capability.

Analytical competitors design effective decision making into their processes to ensure that analytical insights get translated into action and ultimately enhance business performance. They incorporate a way of thinking, putting plans into place, monitoring and correcting those plans, and learning from the results to help shape future actions.[2] For example, U.K. police analysts learned that they could predict from early behaviors which juveniles were likely to become adult criminals. The analysis concluded that if the U.K. police could proactively intervene when kids began to pursue the criminal path, and prevent them from going in that direction, they could dramatically reduce the number of crimes ultimately committed.[3] However, in order for this insight to have any impact on crime rates requires more than awareness; it requires a close collaboration between police, educators, and human services workers to establish programs and practices aimed at eliminating the root causes of crime.

Finally, to ensure that strategy is converted into operational results, organizations must define and monitor metrics that are tied to strategic enterprise objectives, and align individual incentives and metrics with business objectives. (Table 6-2 summarizes the typical situation at each stage of development for each of the three major capability areas.)

Choosing a Path

After an organization has realistically appraised its analytical capabilities, it must next choose which path to pursue. Organizations blessed with top management commitment and passion for analytics can move quickly through the "full steam ahead" path, while the rest are forced to take the slower "prove it" detour.

Full Steam Ahead

A committed, passionate CEO can put the organization on the fast track to analytical competition. To date, firms pursuing this path have usually been start-ups (Google, Yahoo!, Amazon.com, Capital One) whose strategy from the beginning has been to compete on analytics, although occasionally a new CEO at an established firm (such as Gary Loveman of Harrah's or the new general managers at the Oakland A's and Boston

TABLE 6-2

Maturity of analytical capability by stage

STAGE	ORGANIZATION			HUMAN				TECHNOLOGY
	Analytical objective	Analytical process		Skills	Sponsorship	Culture		
1 Analytically impaired	Limited insight into customers, markets, competitors	Doesn't exist		None	None	Knowledge allergic—pride on gut-based decisions		Missing/poor-quality data, multiple defines. Un-integrated systems
2 Localized analytics	Autonomous activity builds experience and confidence using analytics; creates new analytically based insights	Disconnected, very narrow focus		Pockets of isolated analysts (may be in finance, SCM, or marketing/CRM)	Functional and tactical	Desire for more objective data, successes from point use of analytics start to get attention		Recent transaction data unintegrated, missing important information. Isolated BI/analytic efforts
3 Analytical aspirations	Coordinated; establish enterprise performance metrics, build analytically based insights	Mostly separate analytic processes. Building enterprise-level plan		Analysts in multiple areas of business but with limited interaction	Executive—early stages of awareness of competitive possibilities	Executive support for fact-based culture—may meet considerable resistance		Proliferation of BI tools. Data marts/data warehouse established/expands
4 Analytical companies	Change program to develop integrated analytical processes and applications and build analytical capabilities	Some embedded analytics processes		Skills exist, but often not aligned to right level/right role	Broad C-suite support	Change management to build a fact-based culture		High-quality data. Have an enterprise BI plan/strategy, IT processes, and governance principles in place
5 Analytical competitors	Deep strategic insights, continuous renewal and improvement	Fully embedded and much more highly integrated		Highly skilled, leveraged, mobilized, centralized, outsourced grunt work	CEO passion. Broad-based management commitment	Broadly supported fact-based culture, testing and learning culture		Enterprise-wide BI/BA architecture largely implemented

Red Sox in baseball) has led a major organizational transformation with analytics.

For a start-up, the primary challenge on this path is acquiring and deploying the human and financial resources needed to build its analytical capabilities. Established companies face a more complex set of challenges because they already have people, data, processes, technology, and a culture. The existence of these resources is a double-edged sword—they can either provide a head start on building an analytical capability or be a source of resistance to using new methods. If organizational resistance is too great, it may be necessary to take a slower path to build support by demonstrating the benefits of analytics.

The organization going full steam ahead is easily recognized, because the CEO (or other top executive) regularly articulates the burning platform for competing on analytics. He or she consistently invests and takes actions designed to build the organization's strategic analytical capability. At such firms the top priority is integrating analytics into the organization's distinctive capability, with an eye to building competitive differentiation. Success is characterized in enterprise-wide terms; company metrics emphasize corporate performance, such as top-line growth and profitability, rather than departmental goals or ROI.

An executive sponsor planning to follow this path must get the rest of the organization on board. The first step is to set a good example. Executives send a powerful message to the entire organization when they make decisions based on facts, not opinions. They must also demand that subordinates support their recommendations with analytically based insights. Second, they must articulate a clear and urgent need for change. It's always easier, of course, to move an organization in an entirely new direction when it is facing a dramatic crisis. Executives at highly successful companies confide that it is difficult to persuade (or compel) employees to become more analytical when no clear need to change is present.

Third, the CEO must also be able to commit the necessary resources. Seriously ailing companies (though they have a clear mandate to do things differently in order to survive) may lack the resources needed for analytical competition. In such cases, pursuing an analytical strategy is like proposing "wellness sessions" to a patient undergoing cardiac arrest. Those organizations will have to revive themselves before pursuing the full-steam-ahead path to analytical competition.

An organization that makes competing on analytics its top priority can expect to make substantial strides in a year or two. While we are convinced that the full-steam-ahead path is ultimately faster, cheaper, and the way to the greatest benefits, we have found relatively few companies prepared to go down this road. If top management lacks the passion and commitment to pursue analytical competition with full force, it is necessary to prove the value of analytics through a series of smaller, localized projects.

Stage 2: Prove-It Detour

To those already convinced of the benefits of analytical competition, having to avoid the fast track feels like an unnecessary detour. Indeed, this path is much slower and circuitous, and there is a real risk that an organization can remain stalled indefinitely. We estimate that having to "prove it" will add one to three years to the time needed to become an analytical competitor. But executives unwilling to make the leap should take a test-and-learn approach—trying out analytics in a series of small steps.

For organizations taking the detour, analytical sponsors can come from anywhere in the organization. For example, at one consumer packaged goods manufacturer, a new marketing vice president was shocked to discover that the analytical capabilities he took for granted at his former employer did not exist at his new company. Rather than try to garner support for a major enterprise-wide program, he logically chose to start small in his own department, by adopting an analytically based model for planning retail trade promotions. In situations like this, initial applications should often be fairly tactical, small in scale, and limited in scope.

Despite its drawbacks, there are also important advantages to taking the slower path. Any true analytical competitor wants to have a series of experiments and evidence documenting the value of the approach, and the prove-it path helps the organization accumulate that empirical evidence. As managers get more experience using smaller, localized applications, they can gain valuable insights that can be translated into business benefits. Each incremental business insight builds momentum within the organization in favor of moving to higher stages of analytical competitiveness.

There are practical reasons for taking the prove-it road as well. By starting small, functional managers can take advantage of analytics to improve the efficiency and effectiveness of their own departments without having to get buy-in from others. This approach also requires a lower level of initial investment, since stand-alone analytical tools and data for a single business function cost less than any enterprise-wide program.

In stage 2, it is best to keep things simple and narrow in scope. The steps essentially boil down to:

1. Finding a sponsor and a business problem that can benefit from analytics

2. Implementing a small, localized project to add value and produce measurable benefits

3. Documenting the benefits and sharing the news with key stakeholders

4. Continuing to build a string of localized successes until the organization has acquired enough experience and sponsorship to progress to the next stage

An organization can linger in stage 2 indefinitely if executives don't see results, but most organizations are ready to move to the next stage in one to three years. By building a string of successes and carefully collecting data on the results, managers can attract top management attention and executive sponsorship for a broader application of analytics. At that point, they are ready to progress to stage 3.

Table 6-3 summarizes some of the major differences in scope, resources, and approach between the full-steam-ahead and the prove-it paths.

For an example of a company that chose the prove-it path, we will now look at the experiences of an organization that has begun to develop its analytical capabilities. (We have disguised the company and the names of the individuals.)

PulpCo: Introducing Analytics to Combat Competitive Pressure

PulpCo is a successful company engaged in the sale of pulp, paper, and lumber-based products, including consumer goods such as paper cups, industrial products like newsprint, and lumber-based products such as particleboard for residential construction. It has successfully sold these products in the United States and Europe for more than twenty years but has been facing increasing pressure from new entrants from developing

TABLE 6-3

Attributes of two paths to analytical competition

	Full steam ahead	Prove it
Management sponsorship	Top general manager/CEO	Functional manager
Problem set	Strategic/distinctive capability	Local, tactical, wherever there's a sponsor
Measure/demonstrate value	Metrics of organizational performance to analytics— e.g., revenue growth, prof- itability, shareholder value	Metrics of project benefits: ROI, productivity gains, cost savings
Technology	Enterprise-wide	Proliferation of BI tools, inte- gration challenges
People	Centralized, highly elite, skilled	Isolated pockets of excellence
Process	Embedded in process, op- portunity through integration supply/demand	Stand-alone or in functional silo
Culture	Enterprise-wide, large-scale change	Departmental/functional, early adopters

economies, newly competitive European firms, and providers of substi- tute materials for construction and consumer products. The PulpCo management team has been with the company for years; most began their careers working at the mills. Traditionally, analytics have taken a back seat to PulpCo's more intuitive understanding of the industry and its dynamics.

Under increasing competitive pressure, the CEO, at a board mem- ber's urging, broke with long-standing tradition and hired a new CFO from outside the industry. Azmil Yatim, the new CFO, had been lured by PulpCo's scale of operations and major market position. But after a month on the job, he was wondering whether he had made a career mistake. The members of PulpCo's management team behaved as though they had limited awareness of the financial implications of their actions. Major investment decisions were often made on the basis of in- accurate, untested assumptions. In operations, managers had grown used to having to make decisions without the right data. They had an incomplete understanding of their costs for major products such as particleboard, construction lumber, toilet paper, and newsprint. As a result, they made some costly mistakes, from unnecessary capital investments in plants and machinery to poor pricing.

The CFO resolved to improve the financial and decision-making capabilities of the organization. Sensing that chief operating officer (COO) Daniel Ghani, a widely respected insider, would be critical to his efforts, Yatim initially sought his support for a bold and far-ranging change initiative to transform the organization. Ghani rejected it as too radical. But the COO was tired of constantly dealing with one crisis after another, and after talking with Yatim, he began to realize that many of these crises resulted from a lack of accurate financial information, which in turn produced poor decisions. Ghani became convinced that the organization could not afford to continue to make decisions in an analytical vacuum. He urged the CFO to devise a new plan that would make effective use of financial data generated by the company's newly installed enterprise system. Better financial information and control became a shared priority of the two executives.

Using a recent series of embarrassing missteps—including a major customer defection to a key competitor—as a rallying point, the CFO (together with the CIO, who reported to him) gained approval and funding for an initiative to improve financially based insights and decision making. He began by reviewing the skills in the finance function and at the mills and realized that operating managers needed help to leverage the new system. He arranged for formal training and also created a small group of analysts to help managers at the mills use and interpret the data. He also provided training to employees engaged in budgeting and forecasting.

As the CFO began to analyze the new data he was receiving, an unsettling picture emerged. PulpCo was actually losing money on some major accounts. Others that were deemed less strategically valuable were actually far more profitable. Armed with these insights, the CFO and his analysts worked with individual executives to interpret the data and understand the implications. As he did, the executive team became more convinced that they needed to instill more financial discipline and acumen in their management ranks.

A breakthrough occurred when detailed financial analysis revealed that a new plant, already in the early stages of construction, would be a costly mistake. Management realized that the company could add to capacity more cost-effectively by expanding and upgrading two existing plants, and the project was canceled. Managers across the company were shocked, since "everyone knew" that PulpCo needed the new plant and had already broken ground.

The executive team then declared that all major investments under way or planned in the next twelve months would be reviewed. Projects that were not supported by a business case and facts derived from the company's enterprise system would be shut down. New projects would not be approved without sufficient fact-based evidence. Managers scrambled to find data to support their projects. But it wasn't until a new managerial performance and bonus program was introduced that managers really began to take financial analysis seriously.

After a year of concerted effort, initial hiccups, and growing pains, PulpCo is a changed organization. Major financial decisions are aligned with strategic objectives and based on facts. Management is largely positive about the insights gained from better financial analysis and supportive of further analytical initiatives in other parts of the business. Forecasts are more accurate, and managers are better able to anticipate and avoid problems. The culture is no longer hostile to the use of data. Operational managers at the mills and at corporate headquarters have increased their financial acumen and are more comfortable interpreting financial analyses. The use of analytics has begun to spread as the organization's managers realize that better insight into costs and profitability can give them an edge in competitive situations. Inspired by analytical companies such as CEMEX, PulpCo has begun a test program to bypass the lumberyard and deliver products directly to the construction site. Not surprisingly, PulpCo is also enjoying better financial performance.

Initially, PulpCo's CFO just wanted improved financial data for decision making. With limited sponsorship and inadequate systems, the CFO realized that he needed to conduct some experiments and build credibility within the organization before attempting a broader change program. With each success, PulpCo's leadership team became more enthusiastic about using analytics and began to see their broader potential. PulpCo is not an analytical competitor and may never reach stage 5, but today management is enthusiastic about the benefits of analytics and is considering whether it should make the leap to stage 3.

Stage 3: Analytical Aspirations

Stage 3 is triggered when analytics gain executive sponsorship. The executive sponsor becomes an outspoken advocate of a more fact-based culture and builds sponsorship with others on the executive team.

Executive sponsorship is so vital to analytical competition that simply having the right sponsor is enough to move an organization to stage 3 without any improvement in its analytical capabilities. However, those organizations pursuing the prove-it path will have already established pockets of analytical expertise and will have some analytical tools in hand. The risk is that several small groups will have their own analytical fiefdoms, replete with hard-to-integrate software tools, data sets, and practices.

Whether an organization has many analytical groups or none at all, it needs to take a broader, more strategic perspective in stage 3. The first task, then, is to articulate a vision of the benefits expected from analytical competition. Bolstered by a series of smaller successes, management should set its sights on using analytics in the company's distinctive capability and addressing strategic business problems. For the first time, program benefits should be defined in terms of improved business performance and care should be taken to measure progress against broad business objectives. A critical element of stage 3 is defining a set of achievable performance metrics and putting the processes in place to monitor progress. To focus scarce resources appropriately, the organization may create a centralized "business intelligence competency center" to foster and support analytical activities.

In stage 3, companies will launch their first major project to use analytics in their distinctive capability. The application of more sophisticated analytics may require specialized analytical expertise and adding new analytical technology. Management attention to change management is critical because significant changes to businesses processes, work roles, and responsibilities are necessary.

If it hasn't already done so, the IT organization must develop a vision and program plan (an analytical architecture) to support analytical competition. In particular, IT must work more aggressively to integrate and standardize enterprise data in anticipation of radically increased demand from users.

The length of stage 3 varies; it can be as short as a few months or as long as two years. Once executives have committed resources and set a timetable to build an enterprise-wide analytical capability, they are ready to move to the next stage.

BankCo (again, we have disguised the company and other names) is an example of an organization moving from stage 3 toward stage 4.

BankCo: Moving Beyond Functional Silos to Enterprise Analytics

Wealth management has been a hot topic within the banking industry over the last decade, and banks have traditionally been well positioned to offer this service. In-house trust departments have provided advice and services to generations of wealthy clients. But over the past several years, new competitors have emerged. Banks have moved away from using individual investment managers, taking a more efficient but less personalized approach. A trend toward greater regulatory oversight is further transforming the industry. At the same time, customers are more open to alternatives to traditional money management. This confluence of factors threatens bank trust departments' hold on the service of managing individuals' wealth.

At BankCo, the executive vice presidents of marketing, strategy, and relationship management were asked by the bank's senior management team to create a strategic response to this threat. They quickly concluded that significant changes were needed to improve the bank's relationships with its customers. BankCo's trust department assets had declined by 7 percent over two years, despite a positive market that had produced increased assets overall and good performance in individual trust accounts. The decline was attributed to discounting by more aggressive competition and to cannibalism of accounts by the bank's brokerage business. BankCo had tried introducing revamped products to retain customers but with limited success.

As in many banks, each department (retail, brokerage, trust) maintained its own customer data that was not available to outsiders. As a result, executives could not get a complete picture of their clients' relationships throughout the bank, and valuable relationships were jeopardized unnecessarily. For example, one client with a $100 million trust was charged $35 for bouncing a check. When he called his retail banker to complain, he was told initially that his savings account wasn't large enough for the bank to justify waiving the fee.

After analyzing these issues, the team concluded that an enterprise-wide focus on analytics would not only eliminate the majority of these problems but also uncover cross-selling opportunities. The team realized that a major obstacle to building an enterprise-level analytical capability would be resistance from department heads. Their performance measures were based on the assets of their departments, not on enterprise-wide metrics. The bank's senior management team responded by introducing new performance metrics that would assess overall enterprise performance (including measures related to asset size and profitability) and cross-departmental cooperation.

These changes cleared the path for an enterprise-wide initiative to improve BankCo's analytical orientation, beginning with the creation of an integrated and consistent customer database (to the extent permitted by law) as well as coordinated retail, trust, and brokerage marketing campaigns. At the same time, an enterprise-wide marketing analytics group was established to work with the marketing teams on understanding client values and behavior. The group began to identify new market segments and offerings, and to help prioritize and coordinate marketing efforts to high-net-worth individuals. It also began to develop a deeper understanding of family relationships and their impact on individual behavior. By bringing together statisticians and analysts scattered throughout the business, BankCo could deploy these scarce resources more efficiently. As demand quickly outstripped supply, it hired analytical specialists with industry expertise and arranged to use an offshore firm to further leverage its scarce analytical talent.

At first, there were occasional breakdowns in decision-making processes. When a competitor restructured its brokerage pricing, BankCo did not notice until several clients left. On another occasion, an analysis identified a new market segment, and management authorized changes to marketing, but the organization was slow to implement the changes. To overcome these hurdles, process changes were implemented to make sure that decisions were translated into action. Managers received training and tools so that they were equipped to make decisions analytically and understood how to develop hypotheses, interpret data, and make fact-based decisions. As the organization's analytical capabilities improved, these breakdowns became less frequent.

As more tangible benefits began to appear, the CEO's commitment to competing on analytics grew. In his letter to shareholders, he described the growing importance of analytics and a new growth initiative to "outsmart and outthink" the competition. Analysts expanded their work to use propensity analysis and neural nets (an artificial intelligence technology incorporating nonlinear statistical modeling to identify patterns) to target and provide specialized services to clients with both personal and corporate relationships with the bank. They also began testing some analytically enabled new services for trust clients. Today, BankCo is well on its way to becoming an analytical competitor.

Stage 4: Analytical Companies

The primary focus in stage 4 is on building world-class analytical capabilities at the enterprise level. In this stage, organizations implement the plan developed in stage 3, making considerable progress toward building the sponsorship, culture, skills, strategic insights, data, and technology needed for analytical competition. Sponsorship grows from a handful of visionaries to a broad management consensus; similarly, an emphasis on experimentation and analytics pervades the corporate culture. As the organization learns more from each analysis, it obtains a rich vein of new insights and ideas to mine and exploit for competitive advantage. Building analytical capabilities is a major (although not the only) corporate priority.

While there are many challenges at this stage, the most critical one is allocating sufficient attention to managing cultural and organizational changes. We've witnessed many organizations whose analytical aspirations were squelched by open cultural warfare between the "quant jocks" and the old guard. A related challenge is extending executive sponsorship to the rest of the management team. If only one or two executives are committed to analytical competition, interest will immediately subside if they suddenly depart or retire. In one case, the CEO of a financial services firm saw analytical competition as his legacy to the organization he had devoted his life to build. But his successors did not share his enthusiasm, and the analytical systems developed under his leadership quickly fell into disuse.

As each analytical capability becomes more sophisticated, management will gain the confidence and expertise to build analytics into business processes. In some cases, they use their superior insight into customers and markets to automate key decision processes entirely.

In stage 4, many organizations realign their analysts and information workers to place them in assignments that are better suited to their skills. As a company becomes more serious about enterprise-wide analytics, it often draws together the most advanced analysts into a single group to focus on strategic issues. This provides the organization with a critical mass of analysts to focus on the most strategic issues, and provides the analysts with greater job satisfaction and opportunity to develop their skills.

Once an organization has an outstanding analytical capability combined with strategically differentiating analytics embedded into its most critical business processes and has achieved major improvements to its business performance and competitiveness, it has reached the final stage.

ConsumerCo: Everything but "Fire in the Belly"

At a large consumer products company, analytical competition is at stage 4. ConsumerCo has everything in place but a strong executive-level commitment to compete on this basis. It has high-quality data about virtually every aspect of its business, and a capable IT function. It has a group of analysts who are equal to any company's. The analysts have undertaken projects that have brought hundreds of millions of dollars in value to the company. Still, they have to justify their existence by selling individual projects to functional managers.

The CEO of ConsumerCo is a strong believer in product innovation and product-oriented research but not particularly in analytics. The primary advocate for analytics is the COO. Analytics are not discussed in annual reports and analyst calls, though the company does have a culture of fact-based decision making and uses a large amount of market research. ConsumerCo is doing well financially but has been growing primarily through acquisitions. In short, analytics are respected and widely practiced but are not driving the company's strategy. With only a bit more "fire in the belly" from senior executives, it could become a true analytical competitor in a short time.

Stage 5: Analytical Competitors

In stage 5, analytics move from being a very important capability for an organization to the key to its strategy and competitive advantage. Analytical competitors routinely reap the benefits of their enterprise-wide analytical capability. Proprietary metrics, analytics, processes, and data create a strong barrier to competitors, but these companies are always attempting to move the analytical bar further.

Executive commitment and passion for analytical competition in this stage is resolute and widespread. The organization's expertise in analytical competition is discussed in annual reports and in discussions with investment analysts. Internal performance measures and processes reinforce a commitment to scientific objectivity and analytical integrity.

However, analytical competitors must avoid complacency if they are to sustain their competitive advantage. They need to build processes to continually monitor the external environment for signs of change. They must also remain vigilant in order to recognize when changing market conditions require them to modify their assumptions, analytical models, and rules.

We've described a large number of these companies already, so we won't give an example here. Each stage 5 company is different in terms of the strategic capability it emphasizes, the applications it employs, and the path it followed to success. But they have in common an absolute passion for analytics and a resulting strong financial performance.

Progressing Along the Road Map

The path to success with analytics will contain speed bumps along the way. Managers not yet on the full-steam-ahead path may be tempted to either shift resources away from or shut down completely an analytics initiative if business conditions put pressure on the organization. Also, the shift to analytics will most likely require employees to change their decision-making processes. It takes time for the organization to adjust to new skills and behaviors, but without them, no real change can occur. As a result, the most important activity for the leadership team is to keep analytical initiatives on track and to monitor outcomes to ensure that anticipated benefits are achieved.

At every stage of development, companies need to manage outcomes to achieve desired benefits, setting priorities appropriately and avoiding common pitfalls.

Managing for Outcomes

Three types of outcomes are critical to measuring an initiative's performance: behaviors, processes and programs, and financial results. While financial results may be all that matter in the end, they probably won't be achieved without attention to intermediate outcomes.

Behaviors. To a large extent, improved financial outcomes depend on changing employee behaviors. Implementing new analytical insights into pricing, for example, can require thousands of individuals to change their behaviors. Managers and employees may initially believe that their own pricing experience is better than that of any system. Managers have to monitor measures and work with employees who don't comply with policies. Executives have to send out frequent messages to reinforce the desired change of direction.

Processes and programs. Fact-based analyses often require process and program changes to yield results. For example, insights into the best way to persuade wireless customers not to defect to another carrier need to be translated into actions—such as developing a new program to train customer-facing employees.

One way to ensure that insights are incorporated into business processes is to integrate analytics into business applications and work processes. Incorporating analytical support applications into work processes helps employees accept the changes and improves standardization and use. For more advanced analytical competitors, automated decision-making applications can be a powerful way of leveraging strategic insights.

Financial results. It is important to specify the financial outcomes desired from an analytical initiative to help measure its success. Specific financial results may include improved profitability, higher revenues, lower costs, or improved market share or market value. Initially, cost savings are the most common justification for an analytical initiative because it is much easier to specify in advance how costs will be cut. Revenue increases are more difficult to predict and measure but can be modeled with analytical tools and extrapolated from small tests and pilot studies. As an organization's analytical maturity increases, it will be more willing to invest in initiatives targeted at exploiting growth opportunities and generating revenue.

Establishing Priorities

Assuming that an organization already has sufficient management support and an understanding of its desired outcomes, analytical orientation, and decision-making processes, its next step is to begin defining and prioritizing actions. Critical questions managers should use to assess the potential of an analytical initiative are in the box entitled: "Questions to Ask When Evaluating New Analytical Initiatives." Projects with the greatest potential benefit to the organization's distinctive capabilities and competitive differentiation should take precedence. Taking an analytical approach to investment decisions, requiring accountability, and monitoring outcomes will help reinforce the analytical culture and maximize investments where they are likely to have the greatest impact.

A common error is to assume that merely having analytical technology is sufficient to transform an organization. The *Field of Dreams* approach—"If you build it, they will come"—usually disappoints. If you build a data warehouse or a full-blown analytical technical infrastructure without developing the other analytical attributes, the warehouse will just sit there.

Avoiding the Potholes

Since every organization is different, we won't attempt to provide detailed instructions to navigate around all the potential hazards encountered along the road map. Hazards can appear suddenly at any stage of development. However, we can provide guidelines to help make the planning and implementing efforts go as smoothly as possible.

Questions to Ask When Evaluating New Analytical Initiatives

- How will this investment make us more competitive?

- How does the initiative improve our enterprise-wide analytical capabilities?

- What complementary changes need to be made in order to take full advantage of new capabilities, such as developing new or enhanced skills; improving IT, training, and processes; or redesigning jobs?

- Does the right data exist? If not, can we get it? Is the data timely, consistent, accurate, and complete?

- Is the technology reliable? Is it cost-effective? Is it scalable? Is this the right approach or tool for the right job?

First, some missteps are due primarily to ignorance. The most common errors of omission are:

- Focusing excessively on one dimension of analytical capability (e.g., too much technology)

- Attempting to do everything at once

- Investing excessive resources on analytics that have minimal impact on the business

- Investing too much or too little in any analytical capability, compared with demand

- Choosing the wrong problem, not understanding the problem sufficiently, using the wrong analytical technique or the wrong analytical software

- Automating decision-based applications without carefully monitoring outcomes and external conditions to see whether assumptions need to be modified

Of greater concern to many executives is the intentional undermining of analytical competition. Many managers share Benjamin Disraeli's suspicion that there are "lies, damned lies, and statistics."[4] Data analysis has the potential for abuse when employed by the unscrupulous, since statistics, if tortured sufficiently, will confess to anything.[5] Applying objective criteria and data for decision making is highly threatening to any bureaucrat accustomed to making decisions based upon his or her own self-interest. Analytical competition cannot thrive if information is hoarded and analytics manipulated. Executives must relentlessly root out self-serving, manipulated statistics and enforce a culture of objectivity.[6]

Conclusion

This chapter has explored the key attributes of an analytical capability and provided a directional guide to the steps that lead to enhanced analytical capabilities. We wish you rapid movement to the full-steam-ahead path to becoming an analytical competitor. In the next chapter, we will explore ways to successfully manage an organization's commitment to key people who are—or need to be—using analytics.

7

Managing Analytical People

Cultivating the Scarce Ingredient
That Makes Analytics Work

WHEN MOST PEOPLE VISUALIZE business analytics, they think of computers, software, and printouts or screens full of numbers. What they should be envisioning, however, are their fellow human beings. It is people who make analytics work and who are the scarce ingredient in analytical competition.

Analytical Urban Legends

This is contrary to some analytical urban legends, so let us dispel those now. A few years ago, we began hearing extravagant tales of software that would eliminate the need for human analysts. The most popular story involved a data mining episode involving diapers and beer. The gist of the story was that some grocery retailer had turned loose its powerful data mining software on a sales database, and it had come up with an interesting finding. Male customers who came in to buy beer for the weekend also tended to remember that their wives had asked them to buy diapers (some versions of the story switched around the primary shopping intent), so they put both products in their shopping carts. The retailer quickly moved diapers over by the beer (or vice versa), and sales exploded.

We chased this one down, and the most credible version of the story happened at Osco, a drugstore chain. Some of the company's data analysts do dimly remember seeing a correlation between diaper and beer sales in their stores. But the analysts had told the software where and how to look for the relationship; it wasn't just stumbled upon by an enterprising young computer. Most importantly, the finding was deemed an anomaly, and diapers and beer were never put in proximity in the Osco stores (not all of which could even sell beer).

The legend is worth discussing, however, for a few lessons it provides. While data mining software is a wonderful thing, a smart human still needs to interpret the patterns that are identified, decide which patterns merit validation or subsequent confirmation, and translate new insights into recommendations for action. Other smart humans need to actually take action. When we studied more than thirty firms with a strong analytical capability in 2000, we found that a heavy dose of human skills was present at each of the firms, and the analytical competitors we've studied over the past couple of years certainly have lots of smart analysts on board.[1]

The other key lesson of the diapers and beer legend is that analytics aren't enough, even when orchestrated by a human analyst. In order for analytics to be of any use, a decision maker has to make a decision and take action—that is, actually move the diapers and beer together. Since decision makers may not have the time or ability to perform analyses themselves, such interpersonal attributes as trust and credibility rear their ugly heads. If the decision maker doesn't trust the analyst or simply doesn't pay attention to the results of the analysis, nothing will happen and the statistics might as well never have been computed.

We found another good example of this problem in our previous study of analytical capability. We talked to analysts at a large New York bank who were studying branch profitability. The analysts went through a painstaking study of branch profitability in the New York area—identifying and collecting activity-based costs, allocating overheads, and even projecting current cost and revenue trends for each branch into the near future. They came up with a neat, clear, ordered list of all branches and their current and future profitability, with an even neater red line drawn to separate the branches that should be left open from those that should be closed.

What happened? Nary a branch was shut down. The retail banking executive who had asked for the list was mostly just curious about the profitability issue, and he hardly knew the analysts. He knew that there were many political considerations involved in, say, closing the branch in Brooklyn near where the borough president had grown up, even if it was well below the red line. Analytically based actions usually require a close, trusting relationship between analyst and decision maker, and that was missing at the bank. Because of the missing relationship, the analysts didn't ask the right questions, and the executive didn't frame the question for them correctly.

There are really three groups, then, whose analytical skills and orientations are at issue within organizations. One is the senior management team—and particularly the CEO—which sets the tone for the organization's analytical culture and makes the most important decisions. Then there are the professional analysts, who gather and analyze the data, interpret the results, and report them to decision makers. The third group is a diverse collection we will refer to as analytical amateurs, a very large group of "everybody else," whose use of the outputs of analytical processes is critical to their job performance. These could range from frontline manufacturing workers, who have to make multiple small decisions on quality and speed, to middle managers, who also have to make middle-sized decisions with respect to their functions and units. Middle managers in the business areas designated as distinctive capabilities by their organizations are particularly important, because they oversee the application of analytics to these strategic processes. IT employees who put in place the software and hardware for analytics also need some familiarity with the topic. We'll describe each of these groups in this chapter.

Senior Executives and Analytical Competition

As if CEOs and senior executives weren't busy enough already, it is their responsibility to build the analytical orientation and capabilities of their organizations. If the CEO or a significant fraction of the senior executive team doesn't understand or appreciate at least the outputs of quantitative analysis or the process of fact-based decision making, analysts are going to be relegated to the back office, and competition will be based on guesswork and gut feel, not analytics. Fact-based decision making doesn't always involve analytics—sometimes "facts" may be very simple pieces of evidence, such as a single piece of data or a customer survey result—but the desire to make decisions on the basis of what's really happening in the world is an important cultural attribute of analytical competitors.[2]

For an example, take Phil Knight, the founder and chairman of Nike. Knight has always been known as an inspirational but intuitive leader who closely guards the mythical Nike brand. Perhaps needless to say, it didn't take a lot of analytics to come up with the famous "swoosh." At the beginning of 2005, however, Knight brought in William Perez, formerly head of S. C. Johnson & Son, as CEO of Nike. Perez, accustomed to the data-intensive world of Johnson's Wax, Windex, and Ziploc bags, attempted to bring a more analytical style of leadership into Nike. He notes about himself, "I am a data man—I like to know what the facts are. If you come from the world of packaged goods, where data is always valuable, Nike is very different. Judgment is very important. Feel is very important. You can't replace that with facts. But you can use data to guide you."[3]

Perez attempted, for example, to move Nike into middle-tier retail environments, where his data suggested that footwear growth was fastest. In response to arguments from Knight and other Nike executives that such a move would weaken the brand, Perez pointed to companies such as Apple that sell successfully in Wal-Mart without diluting their brands. But these and other clashes eventually led Knight and the board of directors to remove Perez little more than a year later.

If Perez, who was CEO of Nike, couldn't move the culture in a more analytical direction, what chance would a more junior executive have of doing so? Not much. In fact, we found several companies in which fairly senior functional managers—corporate heads of marketing or technology, for example—were trying to bring a more analytical orientation to their firms. One, for example, a senior vice president of sales and marketing at a technology company, was known as a true "data hound," bringing piles of statistical reports to meetings and having perfect command of his own (and other managers') statistics. The sales and marketing organizations slowly began to become more data focused, but the overall company culture continued to emphasize chutzpah and confidence more than correlations. In fact, we didn't find a single company that was a stage 4 or 5 analytical competitor where either the CEO or a majority of the senior management team didn't believe strongly in analytics as a primary competitive resource. Senior executive support is even important at stage 3, when organizations begin to aspire to analytical competition.

Characteristics of Analytical Executives

What are the traits that executives in an analytical competitor should have? A few key ones are described next.

They should be passionate believers in analytical and fact-based decision making. You can't inspire others to change their behavior in a more analytical direction if you're not passionate about the goal. A truly committed executive would demonstrate fact-based and analytical decision making in his or her own decisions and continually challenge the rest of the organization to do the same. For example, whenever Barry Beracha, previously CEO of the private-label baker Earthgrains (which was acquired by Sara Lee Bakery Group), needed to make a decision, he searched to turn up the right data. He insisted that the entire organization needed better data, and led the company to implement a new ERP system to create it. After it was available, he pressed his employees to use it when deciding what products to keep and what customers to serve. He was so passionate about data-based decisions that his employees referred to him as a "data dog"—to his delight.

They should have some appreciation of analytical tools and methods. The senior executives of analytical competitors don't necessarily have to be analytical experts (although it helps!). However, they do need to have an awareness of what kinds of tools make sense for particular business problems, and the limitations of those tools. Just as a politician analyzing polls should know something about confidence intervals, the CEO making a decision about a plant expansion should know something about the statistical and qualitative assumptions that went into predicting demand for the goods the plant will make.

They should be willing to act on the results of analyses. There is little point in commissioning detailed analytics if nothing different will be done based on the outcome. Many firms, for example, are able to segment their customers and determine which ones are most profitable or which are most likely to defect. However, they are reluctant to treat different customers differently—out of tradition or egalitarianism or whatever. With such compunctions, they will have a very difficult time becoming successful analytical competitors—yet it is surprising how often companies initiate analyses without ever acting on them. The "action" stage of any analytical effort is, of course, the only one that ultimately counts.

They should be willing to manage a meritocracy. With widespread use of analytics in a company, it usually becomes very apparent who is performing and who isn't. Those who perform well should be rewarded commensurately with their performance; those who don't perform shouldn't be strung along for long periods. As with customers, when the differences in performance among employees and managers are visible but not acted upon, nothing good results—and better employees may well become disheartened. Of course, the leaders of such meritocratic firms have to live and die by this same analytical sword. It would be quite demoralizing for a CEO to preach the analytical gospel for everyone else but then to make excuses for his or her own performance as an executive.

How Does Analytical Leadership Emerge?

Some organizations' leaders had the desire to compete analytically from their beginning. Amazon.com was viewed by founder Jeff Bezos as competing on analytics from its start. Its concept of personalization was based on statistical algorithms and Web transaction data, and it quickly moved into analytics on supply chain and marketing issues as well. Amazon.com has recently used analytics to explore whether it should advertise on television, and has concluded that it would not be a successful use of its resources. Capital One, Netflix, and Google were also analytical from the beginning because their leaders wanted them so. The visions of the founders of these start-up businesses led to analytical competition.

In other cases, the demand for analytical competition came from a new senior executive arriving at an established company. Gary Loveman at Harrah's, and John Henry and Tom Werner, the new owners of the Boston Red Sox, brought with them an entirely new analytical strategy.

Sometimes the change comes from a new generation of managers in a family business. At the winemaker E. & J. Gallo, when Joe Gallo, the son of one of the firm's founding brothers, became CEO, he focused much more than the previous generation of leaders on data and analysis—first in sales and later in other functions, including the assessment of customer taste. At the National Football League's New England Patriots, the involvement in the team by Jonathan Kraft, a former management consultant and the son of owner Bob Kraft, helped move the team in a more analytical direction in terms of both on-field issues like play selection and team composition and off-field issues affecting the fan experience.

The prime mover for analytical demand doesn't always have to be the CEO. At Procter & Gamble, for example, the primary impetus for more analysis is coming from the firm's two vice chairmen. And Jonathan Kraft is the COO of the Patriots, not the CEO.

In addition to the general characteristics described earlier in the chapter (which are generally relevant for the CEO), there are specific roles that particular executives need to play in analytical competition. Two key roles are the chief financial officer (CFO) and the chief information officer (CIO).

Role of the CFO

The chief financial officer in most organizations will have responsibility for financial processes and information. Therefore, analytical efforts in these domains would also be the CFO's concern. Since most analytical projects should involve some sort of financial information or returns, the CFO is at least a partial player in virtually all of them.

We have found several companies in which the CFO was leading the analytical charge. In order to play that role effectively, however, a CFO would have to focus on analytical domains in addition to finance and accounting. For example, at a large insurance company, the CFO had taken responsibility for analytics related to cost control and management but also monitored and championed analytical initiatives in the claims, actuarial, and marketing areas of the company. He also made it his responsibility to try to establish in the company's employees the right overall balance of intuitive versus analytical thinking.

Another CFO (technically a senior vice president of finance) at a retail company made analytics his primary focus, and they weren't even closely connected to finance. The company had a strong focus on customers and customer orientation, and he played a very active role in developing measures, systems, and processes to advance that capability. The company already had good information and analytics on such drivers of its business as labor, space allocation, advertising, and product assortment. His goal was to add the customer relationship and customer segment information to those factors. Since his role also incorporated working with the external financial community (Wall Street analysts, for example), he was also working on making the company's analytical story well known to the outside world. He also viewed his role as including advocacy of a strong analytical orientation in a culture where it wasn't always emphasized. He noted, "I'm not the only advocate of analytics in the company—I have a number of allies. But I am trying to ensure that we tell our stories, both internally and externally, with numbers and analytics."

At Bank of America, CFO Al de Molina views himself as a major instigator of analytical activity. The bank had tried—and largely failed with—a big data warehouse in the early 1990s, so managers were generally wary of gathering together and integrating data. But in his previous job as head of the treasury function, de Molina felt that in order to accurately assess the bank's risks, it needed to consolidate information about assets and rates across the bank. Since the bank was growing rapidly and was assimilating several acquisitions, integrating the information wasn't easy, but de Molina pushed it anyway. The CFO also has taken responsibility for analytics around U.S. macroeconomic performance. Since it has a wealth of data on the spending habits of American consumers, Bank of America can make predictions on the monthly fluctuations in macroeconomic indicators that drive capital markets. This has obvious beneficial implications for the bank's risks. Both the interest rate risk and the macroeconomic analytics domains are obvious ones for a CFO's focus. De Molina largely defers to other executives where, for example, marketing analytics are concerned.

Role of the CIO

The CEO will have the primary responsibility for changing the culture and the analytical behaviors of employees. But CIOs can help in this regard too. They can work with their executive peers to decide what behaviors are necessary and how to elicit them. At least two CIOs we came across are clearly focused on changing the analytical culture of their organizations. Irving Tyler, formerly CIO of Quaker Chemical Corporation (now at IMS Health, Inc.), provided the results of data analysis and reporting through e-mail alerts for several years to Quaker employees. He believed that the more information was delivered to users, the more it began to shape their ability to solve problems and make decisions based on information rather than intuition. He also worked with other Quaker executives on how the organization made key decisions and solved business problems.

At the telecommunications firm Verizon, the CIO's objective is to create a similar change in analytical culture. Verizon and other firms arising out of the "Bell System" have long been analytically oriented, but decisions were generally made slowly and were pushed up the organizational hierarchy. CIO Shaygan Kheradpir is attempting to change this culture through continual exposure to information. He created a form of continuous scorecard in which hundreds of performance metrics of various types are broadcast to PCs around the company, each occupying the screen for fifteen seconds. The idea is to get everyone—not just senior executives—focused on information and what it means, and to encourage employees at all levels to address any issues that appear in the data. Kheradpir feels that he is beginning to see signs of cultural change from the use of the scorecard.

The CIO may also provide a home and a reporting relationship for specialized analytical experts. Such analysts make extensive use of IT and online data, and they are similar in temperament to other IT people. Some of the analytical competitors where analytical groups report to the office of the CIO include Procter & Gamble, the trucking company Schneider National Inc., and Marriott. Procter & Gamble, for example, has recently consolidated its analytical organizations for operations and supply chain, marketing, and other functions. This will allow a critical mass of analytical expertise to be deployed to address P&G's most critical business issues. The group reports to the CIO and is part of an overall emphasis within the IT function on information and decision making (in fact, the IT function has been renamed "information and decision solutions" at Procter & Gamble).

Of course, the most traditional approach to analytics for CIOs is through technology. This is certainly necessary for CIOs in analytical competitors—although, as the foregoing topics suggest, not sufficient. Chapter 8 discusses analytical technology, and it should certainly be apparent from reading that chapter that an architect and a leader are necessary. Those roles may not have to be played by the CIO, but the person(s) playing them would in all likelihood at least report to the CIO.

CIOs wanting to play an even more valuable analytical role than simply overseeing the technology will focus on the *I* in their titles—the information. Analytical competition, of course, is all about information—do we have the right information, is it truly reflective of our performance, and how do we get people to make decisions based on information? These issues are more complex and multifaceted than buying and managing the right technology, but organizations wishing to compete on analytics will need to master them. Research from one important study suggests that companies focusing on their information orientations perform better than those that address technology alone.[4] The authors of the study argue that *information orientation* consists of information behaviors and values, information management practices, and information technology practices—whereas many CIOs only address the latter category. While that study was not primarily focused on analytics, it's a pretty safe bet that information orientation is highly correlated with analytical success.

What If Executive Commitment Is Lacking?

The enemies of an analytical orientation are decisions based solely on intuition and gut feel. Yet these have always been popular approaches to decision making because of their ease and speed and a belief that gut-feel decisions may be better. As we noted in the last chapter, the presence of a committed, passionate CEO can put the organization on the fast track to analytical competition. But for those organizations without sufficient demand for data and analysis in executive decision making, the obvious question is whether such demand can be stimulated. If there is no senior executive with a strong analytical orientation, must the organization wait for such a manager to be appointed?

If you don't have committed executives, it's going to be difficult to do much as an outright analytical competitor, but you can lay the groundwork for a more analytical future. If you're in a position to influence the IT infrastructure, you can make sure that your transaction systems, data, and business intelligence software are in good shape, which means that they reliably produce data and information that is timely and accurate. If you head a function or unit, you can make headway toward a smaller-scale analytical transformation of your part of the business. If you are really smart, influential, and politically astute, you might even plot an analytical coup and depose your nonanalytical rulers. But needless to say, that's a risky career strategy.

There are approaches that can be taken to stimulate demand for analytics by executives. These would generally be actions on the prove-it detour described in the last chapter. At one pharmaceutical firm where we interviewed several IT executives, there was generally little demand from senior executives for analytical decision making, particularly in marketing. IT managers didn't have access to the decisions marketers were trying to make, and the marketing executives didn't know what data or analysis might be available to support their decisions. However, two external events offered opportunities to build analytical demand. One marketing manager discovered a vendor who showed how sales data could be displayed graphically in terms of geography on an interactive map. The company's IT executives felt that the display technique was relatively simple, and they began to offer similar capabilities to the manager to try to build on his interest and nurture the demand for marketing analytics.

A second opportunity was offered by an external study from a consulting firm. One outcome of the study will be a new set of performance indicators. The IT group plans to seize upon the indicators and will offer more analysis and related data to the management team. These IT managers refuse to wait until more analytically oriented senior executives happen to arrive at the company.

The Analytical Professionals

There is an old joke about analytical professionals. It goes this way:

Question: What did the math PhD say to the MBA graduate?

Answer: Would you like fries with that?

That joke is rapidly becoming obsolete, as math PhD's and other analytical professionals leave fast-food employment to play key roles in helping their companies compete on analytics.

In addition to committed executives, most of the analytical competitors we studied had a group of smart and hardworking analytical professionals within their ranks. It is the job of these professionals to design and carry out experiments and tests, to define and refine analytical algorithms, and to perform data mining and statistical analyses on key data. In most cases, such individuals would have advanced degrees—often PhD's—in such analytical fields as statistics, operations research, logistics, and marketing research. In some cases, where the company's distinctive capabilities involve a specialized field (such as geology for an oil exploration firm), the advanced degree will be in that specialty.

One great example of this type of person we found in our research is Katrina Lane, vice president of channel marketing at Harrah's. Lane has the job of figuring out which marketing initiatives to move through which channels, including direct mail, e-mail, call centers, and so forth. This is a complex field of business that hasn't been taught in most business schools, so Lane has to figure a lot out on her own. Fortunately, she's up to the task. To start with, she has a PhD in experimental physics from Cornell. She was head of marketing for a business unit of the May Department Stores Company and a consultant with McKinsey & Company's marketing and sales practice. How common is such a combination of skills and experience? Not very, which is why assembling a capable group of analytical professionals is never easy. As a recent *BusinessWeek* cover story put it:

> The rise of mathematics is heating up the job market for luminary quants, especially at the Internet powerhouses where new math grads land with six-figure salaries and rich stock deals. Tom Leighton, an entrepreneur and applied math professor at Massachusetts Institute of Technology, says: "All of my students have standing offers at Yahoo! and Google." Top mathematicians are becoming a new global elite. It's a force of barely 5,000, by some guesstimates, but every bit as powerful as the armies of Harvard University MBAs who shook up corner suites a generation ago.[5]

Google, for example, is one of the most desired employers on the planet right now. It offers generous salaries, stock options, and what is reputed to be the best cafeteria food anywhere. Yet UC Berkeley professor Hal Varian, who has worked with Google as a consultant since 2002, notes the difficulty of hiring analytical professionals there: "One point that I think needs more emphasis is the difficulty of hiring in this area. Given the emphasis on data, data warehousing, data mining and the like you would think that this would be a popular career area for statisticians. Not so! The bright ones all want to go into biotech, alas. So it is quite hard to pull the talent together, even for Google."[6]

Varian emphasizes the centrality of analytical employees at Google:

> When I went to Google in May 2002 there was one other person doing "ads-stats." He and I worked to build up a whole team in this area and now we have around 20 people doing analytics, some of which is very

sophisticated indeed. And this is just one group at the company: there are also other groups. The most important factor is that upper management is comfortable with quantitative analysis and encourages its use.[7]

Assuming you can find them, how many of these people are necessary? Of course, the answer depends on what an organization is attempting to do with analytics. In the companies we studied, the numbers range from about a dozen analytical professionals to about a hundred. Procter & Gamble, which resides close to the high end of this range, has analytical professionals supporting a variety of functions, including supply chain and marketing.

How are they organized? Most companies have centralized them to some degree. Procter & Gamble, for example, took analytical groups that had been dispersed around the organization, and combined them to form a new global analytics group as part of the IT organization. The trucking firm Schneider National also has its central analytical group as part of the IT domain. Another logical alternative as an organizational home for these high-powered analysts would be the business function that is the primary competitive thrust for the organization. For example, Harrah's keeps most of its "rocket scientists" (including Katrina Lane) in the marketing department, because customer loyalty programs are the primary orientation of its analytics.

Some analysts of the business intelligence industry have disputed (in articles, blogs, and informal communications) our contention that centralized experts of this type are even desirable. They argue that with the current high level of statistical software available, amateurs can get the job done. We agree that capable amateurs are necessary, and we describe them in the next section of this chapter. However, at the most advanced stages of analytics, extensive knowledge of specialized statistical methods is required. As a result of what we learned about the companies we studied, we believe it is impractical for these advanced skills to be broadly distributed throughout the organization. Most organizations will need to have centralized groups that can perform more sophisticated analyses and set up detailed experiments, and we found them in most of the companies we interviewed. It's unlikely, for example, that a "single echelon, uncapacitated, nonstationary inventory management algorithm," employed by one analytical competitor we studied in the supply chain area, would be developed by an amateur analyst. You don't learn about that sort of thing in a typical MBA program.

Regardless of where the professional analysts are located in their firms, many of the analytical competitors we interviewed stressed the importance of a close and trusting relationship between these analysts and the decision makers. As the head of one group put it, "We're selling trust." The need is for analytical experts who also understand the business in general and the particular business need of a specific decision maker. One company referred to such individuals as "front room statisticians," distinguishing them from "backroom statisticians" who have analytical skills but who are not terribly business oriented and may also not have a high degree of interpersonal skills.

In order to facilitate this relationship, a consumer products firm with an IT-based analytical group hires what it calls *PhD's with personality*—individuals with heavy quantitative skills but also the ability to speak the language of the business and market their work to internal (and, in some cases, external) customers. One typical set of job requirements (listed on Monster.com for a vice president of analytic services at McKesson Corporation) reads:

- Advanced degree in Economics, Statistics, or Operations Research

- Minimum of 8 years experience in data analysis, data management, and internet development

- Demonstrated experience in bridging business analysis and technical development

- Experience in building strategic alliances

- Experience with statistical programming SAS, internet tools

- Demonstrated results orientation and follow-through.[8]

At Quaker Chemical, each business unit has a *business adviser*—an analytical specialist—reporting to the head of the business unit. The role acts as an intermediary between the suppliers (normally the IT organization) and the users (executives) of data and analyses. The advisers not only stimulate demand by showing the business unit how analysis can be useful but, as intermediaries, explain business needs to the suppliers and ensure that business-relevant data and analysis will be provided. At Wachovia Bank, a manager of a customer analytics group described the relationships his group tries to maintain: "We are trying to build our people as part of the business team; we want them sitting at the business table, participating in a discussion of what the key issues are, determining what information the business people need to have, and recommending actions to the business partners. We want this [analytical group] to be more than a general utility, but rather an active and critical part of the business unit's success."9

Other executives who manage or have managed such groups described some of the critical success factors for them in our interviews:

- **Building a sustainable pipeline.** Analytical groups need a pipeline of projects, client relationships, and analytical technologies. The key is not just to have a successful project or two but to create sustainability for the organization over time. It's no good to invest in all these capabilities and have the analytical initiative be in existence for only a few years. However, it takes time to build success stories and to have analytics become part of the mythology of the organization. The stories instill a mind-set in the company so that decision makers have the confidence to act.

- **Relationship to IT.** Even if an analytical group isn't officially part of an IT organization, it needs to maintain a close relationship with it. Analytical competitors often need to "push the frontier" in terms of IT. One analytical group's manager in a consumer products firm said that his group had been early users of supercomputers and multiuser servers and had hosted the first Web site for a product (which got thousands of hits on the first day). Exploration of new information technologies wasn't an official mission for the group but one that the company appreciated. It also helped capture the attention and imagination of the company's senior management team.

- **Governance and funding.** How the group is directed and funded is very critical, according to the executives we interviewed. The key issue is to direct analytical groups at the most important problems of the business. This can be done either by mandate or advice from some form of steering committee, or through the funding process. When steering committees are made up of lower-level executives, the tendency seems to be to suboptimize the use of analytical resources. More senior and strategic members create more strategic priorities for analytical professionals.

Funding can also lead to strategic or tactical targets. One group we interviewed was entirely paid for by corporate overhead, which meant that it didn't have to go "tin cupping" for funding and work on unimportant problems that somehow had a budget. Another group did have to seek funding for each project, and said they had to occasionally go to senior management to get permission to turn down lucrative but less important work.

- **Managing politics.** There are often tricky political issues involved in analytical professionals' work, ranging from whose projects the group works on to what the function is called. One company called its analytical group "decision analysis," only to find that executives objected because they felt it was their job to make decisions. The group then changed its name to "options analysis." It can also be politically difficult simply to employ analysts. As one head of an analytical group put it: "So I go to Market Research and say, 'I have a better way to evaluate advertising expenditures.' They don't necessarily react with joy. It's very threatening to them. It makes it particularly difficult if you are asking them to pay you to make them look bad!"[10]

  Heads of analytical groups have to be sensitive to political issues and try to avoid political minefields. The problem is that people who are good at analytics do not often have patience for corporate politics! Before any analysis, they should establish with the internal client that both client and analyst have no stake in any particular outcome, and they will let the analytical chips fall where they may. CEOs can help their analytical professionals by making it clear that the culture rewards those who make evidence-based decisions, even when they go against previously established policies.

- **Don't get ahead of users.** It's important for analytical professionals to keep in mind that their algorithms and processes must often be implemented by information workers, who may be analytically astute but are not expert statisticians. If the analytics and the resulting conclusions are too complex or laced with arcane statistical terminology, they will likely be ignored. One approach is to keep the analytics as simple as possible or to embed them into systems that hide their complexity. Another is to train users of analytical approaches as much as possible. Schneider's analytics group has offered courses such as "Introduction to Data Analysis" and "Statistical Process Control" for users in various functions at the company. It's not a formal responsibility for the group, but the courses are popular, and the group feels it makes their job easier in the long run.

Offshore or Outsourced Analytical Professionals

With expert analytical professionals in short supply within U.S. and European companies, many companies are beginning to think about the possibility of outsourcing them or even going to India or China to find them. It's certainly true that an increasing number of firms offer "knowledge process outsourcing" in analytical fields including data mining, algorithm development, and quantitative finance. In India, firms such as Evalueserve, Inc. and Genpact (formerly the "captive" offshore group of GE Capital) have substantial practices in these domains. Genpact did work in analytical credit analysis for GE Capital and now also offers services in marketing and sales analytics. Some Indian analysts and firms predict large growth in this area.

However, it is difficult for analysts to develop a trusting relationship with decision makers from several thousand miles away. It is likely that the only successful business models for this type of work will combine onshore and offshore capabilities. Onshore analysts can work closely with decision makers, while offshore specialists can do back-office analytical work. If a particular analytical application can be clearly described by the business owner or sponsor before it is developed, there is a good chance that development of the relevant algorithms could be successfully outsourced or taken offshore.

Analytical Amateurs

Much of the daily work of an analytically focused strategy has to be implemented by people without PhD's in statistics or operations research. A key issue, then, is how much analytical sophistication frontline workers need in order to do their jobs. Of course, the nature and extent of needed skills will vary by the company and industry situations. Some firms, such as Capital One, hire a large number of amateur analysts—people with some analytical background, but mostly not PhD types. At one point, when we looked at open jobs on Capital One's Web site, there were three times as many analyst openings as there were jobs in operations—hardly the usual ratio for a bank. According to its particular analytical orientation, a company simply needs to determine how many analytical amateurs it needs in what positions. Some may verge on being professionals; others may have very limited analytical skills but still have to work in business processes that are heavily based on analytics.

The Boston Red Sox's situation in 2003 that we described in chapter 1 is an example of needing to spread analytical orientations throughout the organization. For more business-oriented examples, we'll describe two organizations that are attempting to compete on supply chain analytics. One, a beer manufacturer, put in new supply chain optimization software to ensure that it manufactured and shipped the right amount of beer at the right time. It even created a new position, "beer flow coordinator," to use the system and oversee the optimization process. Yet the company's managers admitted that the beer flow coordinators didn't have the skills to make the process work. No new people were hired, and no substantial training was done. The new system, at least in its early days, was not being used. The company was expecting, one might say, champagne skills on a beer-skills budget.

At a polymer chemicals company, many of the company's products had become commoditized. Executives believed that it was important to optimize the global supply chain to squeeze maximum value and cost out of it. The complexity of the unit's supply chain had significantly increased over the previous couple of years. Responding to the increased complexity, the organization created a global supply chain organization, members of which were responsible for the movement of products and supplies around the world. In the new organization, someone was responsible for the global supply chain, there were planning groups in the regions, and then planners in the different sites. The greatest challenge in the supply chain, however, involved the people who did the work. The new roles were more complex and required a higher degree of analytical sophistication. The company knew that the people performing the previous supply chain roles didn't have the skills to perform the new analytical jobs, but it kept them anyway. At some point, the company plans to develop an inventory of skills needed and an approach to developing or hiring for them, but thus far the lack of skills remains a bottleneck in the implementation of its new logistical process.

When a company is an analytical competitor, it will need to ensure that a wide variety of employees have some exposure to analytics. Most IT people, for example, should have some sense of what analyses are being performed on data, so that they can ensure that IT applications and databases create and manage data in the right formats for analysis. HR people need to understand something about analytics so that they can hire people with the right kinds of analytical skills. Even the corporate legal staff may need to understand the implications of a firm's approach to analytical and automated decision making in case something goes awry in the process.

Firms that have upgraded the analytical skills of employees and managers are starting to see benefits. For example, at a consumer products firm with an analytical strategy, they're seeing a sea change in middle managers. Upper middle management has analytical expertise, either from mathematical backgrounds or from company experience. Two of the central analytical group's key clients have new managers who are more analytical. They were sought out for their analytical orientations and have been very supportive of analytical competition. The analytical managers are more challenging and drive the professional analyst group to higher levels of performance. The senior management team now has analytical discussions, not political ones.

Tools for Amateurs

One of the issues for amateur analysts is what IT tools they use to deal with analytics. There are three possible choices and none seem ideal. One choice is to give them powerful statistical analysis tools so that they can mine data and create powerful algorithms (which they are unlikely to have the skills to do). A second choice is to have the system simply spit out the right answer: the price that should be charged, the amount of inventory to be shipped, and so on. Yet that option may suboptimize the person's ability to use data and make decisions. The third option, which is by far the most common, is to have amateurs do their analytics on spreadsheets.

Spreadsheets (by which we really mean Microsoft Excel, of course) are the predominant tool by which amateurs manipulate data and perform analytics. They have some strengths, or they wouldn't be so common. They are easy to use (at least the basic capabilities); the row-and-column format is widely understood; and they are inexpensive (since Excel comes bundled with widely used office productivity software). Yet as we point out in chapter 2, spreadsheets are a problematic tool for widespread analytical activity. It's very difficult to maintain a consistent, "one version of the truth" analytical environment across an enterprise with a large number of user-managed spreadsheets. And spreadsheets often have errors. Any firm that embraces spreadsheets as the primary tool for analytical amateurs must have a strong approach to data architecture and strong controls over analytics.

An intermediate approach would be to give amateur analysts the ability to view and analyze data, while still providing a structure for the analytical workflow. Some vendors of business intelligence software make such a workflow available. They allow the more analytically sophisticated users to do their own visual queries, while letting less sophisticated users observe and understand some of the analytical processes being followed.

Automated Decision Making

Another critical factor involving analytical amateurs that must be addressed is how highly automated a solution for a given problem should be.[11] As automating more and more decisions becomes possible, it is increasingly important for organizations to address which decisions have to be made by people and which can be computerized. Automated decision applications are typically triggered without human intervention: they sense online data or conditions, apply analytical algorithms or codified knowledge (usually in the form of rules), and make decisions—all with minimal human intervention.

Fully automated applications are configured to translate high-volume or routine decisions into action quickly, accurately, and efficiently because they are embedded into the normal flow of work. Among analytical competitors, we found automated decision technologies being used for a variety of operational decisions, including extension of credit, pricing, yield management, and insurance underwriting. If experts can readily codify the decision rules and if high-quality data is available, the conditions are ripe for automating the decision.[12] Bank credit decisions are a good example; they are repetitive, are susceptible to uniform criteria, and can be made by drawing on the vast supply of consumer credit data that is available.

Still, some types of decisions, while infrequently made, lend themselves well to automation—particularly cases where decision speed is crucial. For example, in the electrical energy grid, quick and accurate shutoff decisions at the regional level are essential to avert a systemwide failure. The value of this rapid response capability was clearly demonstrated during the summer of 2003, when automated systems in some regions of the United States were able to respond quickly to power surges to their networks by shutting off or redirecting power to neighboring lines with spare capacity. It is also evident in some of today's most advanced emergency response systems, which can automatically decide how to coordinate ambulances and emergency rooms across a city in the event of a major disaster.

Automated decision-making applications have some limitations, however. Even when fully automating a decision process is possible, fiduciary, legal, or ethical issues may still require a responsible person to play an active role. Also, automated decisions create some challenges for the organization. Because automated decision systems can lead to the reduction of large staffs of information workers to just a handful of experts, management must focus on keeping the right people—those with the highest possible skills and effectiveness.

The Override Issue

A related issue is how amateurs should deal with automated decisions with which they don't agree. Some firms, such as Harrah's, discourage employees from overriding their automated analytical systems, because they have evidence that the systems get better results than people do. A hotel manager, for example, is not allowed to override the company's revenue management system, which figures out the ideal price for a room based on availability trends and the loyalty level of the customer.

Marriott, as we've described, has similar revenue management systems for its hotels. Yet the company actually encourages its regional "revenue leaders" to override the system. It has devised ways for regional managers to introduce fast-breaking, anomalous information when local events unexpectedly affect normal operating data—such as when Houston was inundated with Hurricane Katrina evacuees. The revenue management system noticed that an unexpected number of people wanted Marriott rooms in Houston in August, and on its own it would have raised rates. But Marriott hardly wanted to discourage evacuees from staying in its Houston-area hotels, so revenue leaders overrode the system and lowered rates. Marriott executives say that such an approach to overriding automated systems is part of a general corporate philosophy. Otherwise, they argue, they wouldn't have bothered to hire and train analytically capable people who make good decisions.

Why these two different philosophies? There are different systems involved, different business processes, and different levels of skill. Companies with a high skill level among analytical amateurs may want to encourage overrides when people think they know more than the system. Partners HealthCare's physicians, who are often also professors at Harvard Medical School, are encouraged to override automated decision systems when doing so is in the best interest of the patient. With such highly trained experts involved in the process, the best result is probably from the combination of humans and automated decision rules.

Companies that feel they have most of the variables covered in their automated analytical models—and that have lower levels of analytical skills at the front line—may prefer to take a hard line on overrides. To some degree, the question can be decided empirically—if overrides usually result in better decisions, they should be encouraged. If not, they should be prohibited most of the time. If a company does decide to allow overrides, it should develop some systematic means of capturing the reasons for them so that the automated model might be improved through the input. At Partners, for example, physicians are asked to give a reason when they override the automated system, and physicians who constantly override a particular system recommendation are interviewed about their reasoning.

Whatever the decision on people versus automation, the key message of this chapter is that the human resource is perhaps the most important capability an analytical competitor can cultivate. When we asked analytical competitors what's hard about executing their strategies, most said it was getting the right kinds of analytical people in sufficient numbers. Hardware and software alone can't come close to creating the kinds of capabilities that analytical strategies require. Whether we're talking about senior executives, analytical professionals, or frontline analytical amateurs, everyone has a job to do in making analytical competition successful.

8

THE ARCHITECTURE OF BUSINESS
INTELLIGENCE

Aligning a Robust Technical Environment
with Business Strategies

MOVIEGOERS MIGHT UNDERSTANDABLY have the impression that
the technical challenges of capturing and analyzing large amounts of
data have already been solved. In many Hollywood films, unlimited
data is accessible to anyone with a laptop and knowledge of a few pass-
words (often obtained in seconds through adroit hacking).

Fortunately for our privacy, however, it's not quite that easy.

Certainly, it has become technically feasible to capture and store
huge quantities of data. The numbers are hard to absorb for all but the
geekiest, as data volumes have grown from megabytes to gigabytes to
terabytes (a trillion bytes); some corporate databases are rapidly ap-
proaching one petabyte (a quadrillion bytes). While low-end computers
and servers lack the power and capacity to handle the volumes of data
required for analytical applications, high-end 64-bit processors and
specialty "data appliances" can quickly churn through virtually unfath-
omable amounts of data.

However, while organizations have more data than ever at their dis-
posal, they rarely know what to do with it. The data in their systems is
often like the box of photos you keep in your attic, waiting for the "someday" when you impose meaning on the chaos. Further, the unpalatable

truth is that most IT departments strain to meet minimal service de-mands and invest inordinate resources in the ongoing support and maintenance of basic transactional capabilities. Unlike the analytical vanguard, even companies with sound transaction systems struggle with relatively prosaic issues such as data cleansing when they try to in-tegrate data into analytical applications. In short, while improvements in technology's ability to store data can be astonishing, most organiza-tions' ability to manage, analyze, and apply data has not kept pace.

Companies that compete on analytics haven't solved all these prob-lems entirely, but they are a lot better off than their competition. In this chapter, we identify the technology, data, and governance processes needed for analytical competition. We also lay out the components that make up the core of any organization's business intelligence architec-ture and forecast how these elements are likely to evolve over time.

Analytics and the Architecture of Business Intelligence

Every company with serious analytical aspirations has an involved, committed IT organization behind it. For example, by capturing propri-etary data or embedding proprietary analytics into business processes, the IT department helps develop and sustain an organization's compet-itive advantage.

But it is important to understand that this work cannot be delegated to IT alone. Determining the technical capabilities needed for analytical competition requires a close collaboration between IT and business managers. This is a principle that companies like Progressive Insur-ance understand fully. Glen Renwick, CEO of Progressive Insurance and former head of IT, understands how critical it is to align IT with business strategy: "Here at Progressive we have technology leaders working arm in arm with business leaders who view their job as solving business problems. And we have business leaders who are held ac-countable for understanding the role of technology in their business. Our business plan and IT are inextricably linked because their job ob-jectives are."[1]

We found this same level of IT/business alignment at many analyti-cal competitors.

Analytical competitors also establish a set of guiding principles to ensure that their IT investments reflect corporate priorities. The princi-ples may include statements such as:

- The risk associated with conflicting information sources must be reduced.

- Applications should be integrated, since analytics increasingly draw data that crosses organizational boundaries.

- Analytics must be enabled as part of the organization's strategy and distinctive capability.

Responsibility for getting the data, technology, and processes right is the job of the *IT architect.* This executive (working closely with the CIO) must determine how the components of the IT infrastructure (hardware, software, and networks) will work together to provide the data, technology, and support needed by the business. This task is easier for start-ups such as Netflix that can create their IT environment with analytical competition in mind from the outset. In large established organizations however, the IT infrastructure can sometimes appear to have been constructed in a series of weekend handyman jobs. It does the job it was designed to do but is apt to create problems whenever it is applied to another purpose.

To make sure the IT environment fully addresses an organization's needs at each stage of analytical competition, companies must incorporate analytics and other business intelligence technologies into their overall IT architecture. (Refer to the box "Data and IT Capability by Stage of Analytical Competition.")

As we pointed out in chapter 1, technologists use the term *business intelligence* (often shortened as BI) to encompass not only analytics—the use of data to analyze, forecast, predict, optimize, and so on—but also the processes and technologies used for collecting, managing, and reporting decision-oriented data. The *business intelligence architecture* (a subset of the overall IT architecture) is an umbrella term for an enterprise-wide set of systems, applications, and governance processes that enable sophisticated analytics, by allowing data, content, and analyses to flow to those who need it, when they need it. (Refer to the box "Signposts of Effective IT for Analytical Competition.")

"Those who need it" will include statisticians of varying skills, information workers, functional heads, and top management. The BI architecture must be able to quickly provide users with reliable, accurate information and help them make decisions of widely varying complexity. It also must make information available through a variety of distribution

---

Data and IT Capability by Stage of Analytical Competition

Established companies typically follow an evolutionary process to develop their IT analytical capabilities.

Stage 1. The organization is plagued by missing or poor-quality data, multiple definitions of its data, and poorly integrated systems.

Stage 2. The organization collects transaction data efficiently but often lacks the right data for better decision making.

Stage 3. The organization has a proliferation of business intelligence tools and data marts, but most data remains unintegrated, nonstandardized, and inaccessible.

Stage 4. The organization has high-quality data, an enterprise-wide analytical plan, IT processes and governance principles, and some embedded or automated analytics.

Stage 5. The organization has a full-fledged analytic architecture that is enterprise-wide, fully automated and integrated into processes, and highly sophisticated.

---

channels, including traditional reports, ad hoc analysis tools, corporate dashboards, spreadsheets, e-mails, and pager alerts. This task is often daunting: Amazon.com, for example, spent more than ten years and a billion dollars building, organizing, and protecting its data warehouses.[2]

Complying with legal and regulatory reporting requirements is another activity that depends on a robust BI architecture. The Sarbanes-Oxley Act of 2002, for example, requires executives, auditors, and other users of corporate data to demonstrate that their decisions are based on trustworthy, meaningful, authoritative, and accurate data. It also requires them to attest that the data provides a clear picture of the business, major trends, risks, and opportunities.

Conceptually, it's useful to break the business intelligence architecture into its six elements (refer to figure 8-1):

- Data management that defines how the right data is acquired and managed

- Transformation tools and processes that describe how the data is extracted, cleaned, transmitted, and loaded to "populate" databases

---

Signposts of Effective IT for Analytical Competition

- Analysts have direct, nearly instantaneous access to data.

- Information workers spend their time analyzing data and understanding its implications rather than collecting and formatting data.

- Managers focus on improving processes and business performance, not culling data from laptops, reports, and transaction systems.

- Managers never argue over whose numbers are accurate.

- Data is managed from an enterprise-wide perspective throughout its life cycle, from its initial creation to archiving or destruction.

- A hypothesis can be quickly analyzed and tested without a lot of manual behind-the-scenes preparation beforehand.

- Both the supply and demand sides of the business rely on forecasts that are aligned and have been developed using a consistent set of data.

- High-volume, mission-critical decision-making processes are highly automated and integrated.

- Data is routinely and automatically shared between the company and its customers and suppliers.

- Reports and analyses seamlessly integrate and synthesize information from many sources.

- Rather than have data warehouse or business intelligence initiatives, companies manage data as a strategic corporate resource in all business initiatives.

- Repositories that organize data and metadata (information about the data) and store it for use

- Applications and other software tools used for analysis

- Presentation tools and applications that address how information workers and non-IT analysts will access, display, visualize, and manipulate data

- Operational processes that determine how important administrative activities such as security, error handling, "auditability," archiving, and privacy are addressed.

FIGURE 8-1

Business intelligence architecture

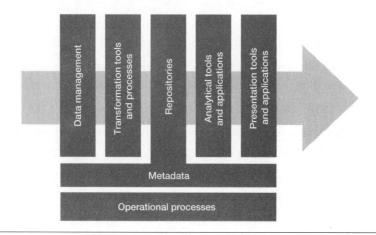

We'll look at each element in turn, with particular attention to data since it drives all the other architectural decisions.

Data Management

The goal of a well-designed data management strategy is to ensure that the organization has the right information and uses it appropriately. Large companies invest millions of dollars in systems that snatch data from every conceivable source. Systems for enterprise resource planning, customer relationship management, and point-of-sale transactions, among others, ensure that no transaction or exchange occurs without leaving a mark. Many organizations also purchase externally gathered data from syndicated providers such as IRI and ACNielsen in consumer products and IMS Health in pharmaceuticals.

In this environment, data overload can be a real problem for time-stressed executives. But the greatest data challenge facing companies is "dirty" data: information that is inconsistent, fragmented, and out of context. Even the best companies often struggle to address their data issues. We found that companies that compete on analytics devote extraordinary attention to data management processes and governance. Capital One, for example, estimates that 25 percent of its IT organization works on data issues—an unusually high percentage compared with other firms.

There's a significant payoff for those who invest the effort to master data management. For example, Continental Airlines integrates 10 TB (terabytes) of data from twenty-five operational systems into its data warehouse. The data is used in analytical applications for both real-time alerts and long-range strategic analysis. Alerts notify customer agents of delays in incoming flights and identify incoming frequent-flier customers who are assigned alternative flights if they are unlikely to make their connections. Marketing analysts use other data collected by the systems to study customer and pricing trends, and logistical analysts plan the optimal positioning of planes and crews. The company estimates that it has saved more than $250 million in the first five years of its data warehousing and business intelligence activities—representing an ROI of over 1,000 percent.[3]

To achieve the benefits of analytical competition, IT and business experts must tackle their data issues by answering five questions:

- Data relevance: What data is needed to compete on analytics?

- Data sourcing: Where can this data be obtained?

- Data quantity: How much data is needed?

- Data quality: How can the data be made more
                      accurate and valuable for analysis?

- Data governance: What rules and processes are needed to
                      manage data from its creation through its
                      retirement?

What Data Is Needed to Compete on Analytics?

The question behind this question is, What data is most valuable for competitive differentiation and business performance? To answer, executives must have a clear understanding of the organization's distinctive capability, the activities that support that capability, and the relationship between an organization's strategic and operational metrics and business performance. Many of the companies described in this book have demonstrated the creative insight needed to make those connections.

But ensuring that analysts have access to the right data can be difficult. Sometimes a number is needed: the advent of credit scores made the mortgage-lending business more efficient by replacing qualitative assessments of consumer creditworthiness with a single, comparative metric. But not everything is readily reducible to a number. An employee's performance rating doesn't give as complete a picture of his work over a year as a manager's written assessment. The situation is complicated when business and IT people blame each other when the wrong data is collected or the right data is not available. Studies such as the one conducted by McDonald and Blosch in Gartner's 2006 CIO survey repeatedly show that IT executives believe business managers do not understand what data they need.[4] And surveys of business managers reflect their belief that IT executives lack the business acumen to make meaningful data available. While there is no easy solution to this problem, the beginning of the solution is for business leaders and IT managers to pledge to work together on this question. Without such cooperation, an organization's ability to gather the data it needs to compete analytically is doomed.

A related issue requiring business and IT collaboration is defining relationships among the data used in analysis. Considerable business expertise is required to help IT understand the potential relationships in the data for optimum organization. The importance of this activity can be seen in an example involving health care customers. From an insurance company's perspective, they have many different customers—their corporate customers that contract for policies on behalf of their employees, individual subscribers, and members of the subscribers' families. Each individual has a medical history and may have any number of medical conditions or diseases that require treatment. The insurance company and each person covered by a policy also have relationships with a variety of service providers such as hospitals, HMOs, and doctors. A doctor may be a general practitioner or a specialist. Some doctors will work with some hospitals or insurers but not others. Individuals can have insurance from multiple providers, including the government, that need to be coordinated. Without insight into the nature of these relationships, the data's usefulness for analytics is extremely limited.

Where Can This Data Be Obtained?

Data for business intelligence originates from many places, but the crucial point is that it needs to be managed through an enterprise-wide infrastructure. Only by this means will it be streamlined, consistent, and scalable throughout the organization. Having common applications and data across the enterprise is critical because it helps yield a "consistent version of the truth," an essential goal for everyone concerned with analytics. While it is possible to create such an environment by ex post facto integration and the transformation of data from many systems, companies are well advised to update and integrate their processes and transaction systems before embarking on this task.

For internal information, the organization's enterprise systems are a logical starting point. For example, an organization wishing to optimize its supply chain might begin with a demand-planning application. However, it can be difficult to analyze data from transaction systems (like inventory control) because it isn't defined or framed correctly for management decisions. Enterprise systems—integrated software applications that automate, connect, and manage information flows for business processes such as order fulfillment—often help companies move along the path toward analytical competition: they provide consistent, accurate, and timely data for such tasks as financial reporting and supply chain optimization. Vendors increasingly are embedding analytical capabilities into their enterprise systems so that users can develop sales forecasts and model alternative solutions to business problems.

In addition to corporate systems, an organization's personal computers and servers are loaded with data. Databases, spreadsheets, presentations, and reports are all sources of data. Sometimes these sources are stored in a common knowledge management application, but they are often not available across the entire organization.

For external information, managers can purchase data from firms that provide financial and market information, consumer credit data, and market measurement. Governments at all levels are some of the biggest information providers, and company Web sites to which customers and suppliers can contribute are another powerful resource. Data can also come from the sources popularized in the movies: e-mail, voice applications, images (maps and photos available through the Internet), and biometrics (fingerprints and iris identification). The further the data type is from standard numbers and letters, however, the harder it is to integrate with other data and analyze.

More data about the physical world, through sensor technology and radio frequency identification (RFID) tags, is becoming available as well. Some packages can communicate their physical condition—for example, a case of wine could be monitored to see whether it is being kept at the proper temperature.

It can be difficult and expensive to capture some highly valuable data. (In some cases, it might even be illegal—for example, sensitive customer information or competitor intelligence about new product plans or pricing strategies.) Analytical competitors adopt innovative approaches to gain permission to collect the data they need. As we described in chapter 3, Progressive Insurance's TripSense program offers discounts to customers who agree to install a device that collects data about their driving behavior. Former CEO Peter Lewis sees this capability as the key to more accurate pricing and capturing the most valuable customers: "It's about being able to charge them for whatever happens instead of what they [customers] say is happening. So what will happen? We'll get all the people who hardly ever drive, and our competitors will get stuck with the higher risks."[5]

How Much Data Is Needed?

In addition to gathering the right data, companies need to collect a lot of it in order to distill trends and predict behavior. What's "a lot"? To put the 583 TB in Wal-Mart's databases into perspective, consider that in 2006, 20 TB was roughly the size of the U.S. Library of Congress's print collection.[6] Fortunately, the technology and techniques for mining and managing large volumes of data are making enormous strides.

Two pitfalls must be balanced against this need for large quantities of data. First, companies have to resist the temptation to collect all possible data "just in case." For one thing, if executives have to wade through digital mountains of irrelevant data, they'll give up and stop using the tools at hand. For another, it can't be done: data hoarders quickly learn that they can't collect everything, and that even if they try, the costs outweigh the benefits. The fundamental issue comes back, again, to knowing what drives value in an organization; this understanding will prevent companies from collecting data indiscriminately.

A related second pitfall: companies should avoid collecting data that is easy to capture but not necessarily important. Many IT executives advocate this low-hanging-fruit approach because it relieves them of responsibility for determining what information is valuable to the business. For example, many companies fall into the trap of providing managers with data that is a by-product of transaction systems, since that is what is most readily available. Perhaps emerging technologies will someday eliminate the need to separate the wheat from the chaff. But until they do, applying intelligence to the process is necessary to avoid data overload.

How Can We Make Data More Valuable?

Quantity without quality is a recipe for failure. Executives are aware of the problem: in a survey of the challenges organizations face in developing a business intelligence capability, data quality was second only to budget constraints.[7] Even analytical competitors struggle with data quality.

Organizations tend to store their data in hard-walled, functional silos. As a result, the data is generally a disorganized mess. For most organizations, differing definitions of key data elements such as *customer* or *product* add to the confusion. When Canadian Tire Corporation, for example, set out to create a structure for its data, it found that the company's data warehouse could yield as many as six different numbers for inventory levels. Other data was not available at all, such as comparison sales figures for certain products sold in its 450-plus stores throughout Canada. Over several years, the company created a plan to collect new data that fit the company's analytical needs.[8]

Several characteristics increase the value of data:

- **It is correct.** While some analyses can get by with ballpark figures and others need precision to several decimal points, all must be informed by data that passes the credibility tests of the people reviewing it.

- **It is complete.** The definition of *complete* will vary according to whether a company is selling cement, credit cards, season tickets, and so on, but completeness will always be closely tied to the organization's distinctive capability.

- **It is current.** Again, the definition of *current* may vary; for some business problems, such as a major medical emergency, data must be available instantly to deploy ambulances and emergency personnel in real time (also known as *zero latency*); for most other business decisions, such as a budget forecast, it just needs to be updated periodically—daily, weekly, or monthly.

- **It is consistent.** In order to help decision makers end arguments over whose data is correct, standardization and common definitions must be applied to it. Eliminating redundant data reduces the chances of using inconsistent or out-of-date data.

- **It is in context.** When data is enriched with *metadata* (usually defined as structured data about data), its meaning and how it should be used become clear.

- **It is controlled.** In order to comply with business, legal, and regulatory requirements for safety, security, privacy, and "auditability," it must be strictly overseen.

What Rules and Processes Are Needed to Manage the Data from Its Acquisition Through Its Retirement?

Each stage of the data management life cycle presents distinctive technical and management challenges that can have a significant impact on an organization's ability to compete on analytics.[9]

- **Data acquisition.** Creating or acquiring data is the first step. For internal information, IT managers should work closely with business process leaders. The goals include determining what data is needed and how to best integrate IT systems with business processes to capture good data at the source.

- **Data cleansing.** Detecting and removing data that is out of date, incorrect, incomplete, or redundant is one of the most important, costly, and time-consuming activities in any business intelligence technology initiative. We estimate that between 25 percent and 30 percent of a BI initiative typically goes toward initial data cleansing. IT's role is to establish methods and systems to collect, organize, process, and maintain information, but data cleansing is the responsibility of everyone who generates or uses data.

- **Data organization and storage.** Once data has been acquired and cleansed, processes to systematically extract, integrate, and synthesize it must be established. The data must then be put into the right repository and format so that it is ready to use (see the discussion of repositories later in the chapter).

- **Data maintenance.** After a repository is created and populated with data, managers must decide how and when the data will be updated. They must create procedures to ensure data privacy, security, and integrity (protection from corruption or loss via human error, software virus, or hardware crash). And policies and processes must also be developed to determine when and how data that is no longer needed will be saved, archived, or retired. Some analytical competitors have estimated that they spend $500,000 in ongoing maintenance for every $1 million spent on developing new business intelligence technical capabilities.

Once an organization has addressed data management issues, the next step is to determine the technologies and processes needed to capture, transform, and load data into a data warehouse.

Transformation Tools and Processes

For data to become usable by managers, it must first go through a process known in IT-speak as ETL, for extract, transform, and load. While extracting data from its source and loading it into a repository are fairly straightforward tasks, cleaning and transforming data is a bigger issue.

In order to make the data in a warehouse decision-ready, it is necessary to first clean and validate it using business rules that use data cleansing tools such as Trillium. (For example, a simple rule might be to have a full nine-digit ZIP code for all U.S. addresses.) Transformation procedures define the business logic that maps data from its source to its destination. Both business and IT managers must expend significant effort in order to transform data into usable information. While automated tools from vendors such as Informatica Corporation, Ab Initio Software Corporation, and Ascential Software can ease this process, considerable manual effort is still required. Informatica's CEO Sohaib Abbasi estimates that "for every dollar spent on integration technology, around seven to eight dollars is spent on labor [for manual data coding]."[10]

Transformation also entails standardizing data definitions to make certain that business concepts have consistent, comparable definitions across the organization. For example, a "customer" may be defined as a company in one system but as an individual placing an order in another. It also requires managers to decide what to do about data that is missing. Sometimes it is possible to fill in the blanks using inferred data or projections based on available data; at other times, it simply remains missing and can't be used for analysis. These mundane but critical tasks require an ongoing effort, because new issues seem to constantly arise.

Repositories

Organizations have several options for organizing and storing their analytical data:

- *Data warehouses* are databases that contain integrated data from different sources and are regularly updated. They contain time-series (historical) data to facilitate the analysis of business performance over time. A data warehouse may be a module of an enterprise system or an independent database. Some companies also employ a staging database that is used to get data from many different sources ready for the data warehouse.

- A *data mart* can refer to a separate repository or to a partitioned section of the overall data warehouse. Data marts are generally used to support a single business function or process and usually contain some predetermined analyses so that managers can independently slice and dice some data without having statistical expertise. Some companies that did not initially see the need for a separate data warehouse created a series of independent data marts or analytical models that directly tapped into source data. One large chemical firm, for example, had sixteen data marts. This approach is rarely used today, because it results in balkanization of data and creates maintenance problems for the IT department. Data marts, then, should only be used if the designers are confident that no broader set of data will ever be needed for analysis.

- A *metadata repository* contains technical information and a data definition, including information about the source, how it is calculated, bibliographic information, and the unit of measurement. It may include information about data reliability, accuracy, and instructions on how the data should be applied. A common metadata repository used by all analytical applications is critical to ensure data consistency. Consolidating all the information needed for data cleansing into a single repository significantly reduces the time needed for maintenance.

Once the data is organized and ready, it is time to determine the analytic technologies and applications needed.

Analytical Tools and Applications

Choosing the right software tools or applications for a given decision depends on several factors. The first task is to determine how thoroughly decision making should be embedded into business processes. Should there be a human who reviews the data and analytics and makes a decision, or should the decision be automated and something that happens in the natural process workflow? If the answer is the latter, there are technologies that both structure the workflow and provide decision rules—either quantitative or qualitative—to make the decision. We addressed this issue from a human perspective in chapter 7.

The next decision is whether to use a third-party application or create a custom solution. A growing number of functionally or industry-specific business applications, such as capital-budgeting or mortgage-pricing models, now exist. Enterprise systems vendors such as Oracle and SAP are building more (and more sophisticated) analytical applications into their products. According to IDC, projects that implement a packaged analytical application yield a median ROI of 140 percent, while custom development using analytical tools yields a median ROI of 104 percent. The "make or buy" decision hinges upon whether a packaged solution exists and whether the level of skill required exists within the organization.[11]

But there are also many powerful tools for data analysis that allow organizations to develop their own analyses (see the box "Analytical Technologies"). Major players such as Business Objects and SAS offer product suites consisting of integrated tools and applications. Some tools are designed to slice and dice or to drill down to predetermined views of the data, while others are more statistically sophisticated. Some tools can accommodate a variety of data types, while others are more limited (to highly structured data or textual analysis, for example). Some tools extrapolate from historical data, while others are intended to seek out new trends or relationships.

Whether a custom solution or off-the-shelf application is used, the business IT organization must accommodate a variety of tools for different types of data analysis (see the box "Analytical Technologies" for current and emerging analytical tools). Employees naturally tend to prefer familiar products, such as a spreadsheet, even if is ill suited for the analysis to be done. Another problem is that without an overall architecture to guide tool selection, excessive technological proliferation can result. In a 2005 survey, respondents from large organizations reported that their organizations averaged thirteen business intelligence tools from an average of 3.2 vendors.[12] Even well-managed analytical competitors often have a large number of software tools. In the past, this was probably necessary, because different vendors had different capabilities—one might focus on financial reporting, another on ad hoc query, and yet another on statistical analysis. While there is still variation among vendors, the leading providers have begun to offer business intelligence suites with stronger, more integrated capabilities.

Analytical Technologies

Typical Analytical Technologies

Executives in organizations that are planning to become analytical competitors should be familiar with the key categories of analytical software tools:

Spreadsheets such as Microsoft Excel are the most commonly used analytical tools because they are easy to use and reflect the mental models of the user. Managers and analysts use them for "the last mile" of analytics—the stage right before the data is presented in report or graphical form for decision makers. But too many users attempt to use spreadsheets for tasks for which they are ill suited, leading to errors or incorrect conclusions. Even when used properly, spreadsheets are prone to human error; more than 20 percent of spreadsheets have errors, and as many as 5 percent of all calculated cells are incorrect.[13] To minimize these failings, managers have to insist on always starting with accurate, validated data and that spreadsheet developers have the proper skills and expertise to develop models.

Online analytical processors are generally known by their abbreviation, OLAP, and are used for semistructured decisions and analyses. While a relational database (or RDBMS)—in which data is stored in related tables—is a highly efficient way to organize data for transaction systems, it is not particularly efficient when it comes to analyzing array-based data (data that is arranged in cells like a spreadsheet), such as time series.

OLAP tools are specifically designed for multidimensional, array-based problems. They organize data in "data cubes" to enable analysis across time, geography, product lines, and so on. Data cubes are simply collections of data in three variables or more that are prepackaged for reporting and analysis; they can be thought of as multidimensional spreadsheets. While spreadsheet programs like Excel have a maximum of three dimensions (down, across, and worksheet pages), OLAP models can have seven or more. As a result, they require specialized skills to develop, although they can be created by "power users" familiar with their capabilities. Unlike traditional spreadsheets, OLAP tools must deal with data proliferation, or the models quickly become unwieldy. For complex queries, OLAP tools are reputed to produce an answer in around 0.1 percent of the time that it would take for the same query to be answered using relational data. Business Objects and Cognos are among the leading vendors in this category.

Statistical or quantitative algorithms enable analytically sophisticated managers or statisticians to analyze data. The algorithms process quantitative data to arrive at an optimal target such as a price or a loan amount. In the 1970s, companies such as SAS and SPSS introduced packaged computer applications that made statistics much more accessible. Statistical algorithms also encompass predictive modeling applications, optimization, and simulations.

Rule engines process a series of business rules that use conditional statements to address logical questions—for example, "If the applicant for a motorcycle insurance policy is male and under 25, and does not either own his own home or have a graduate degree, do not issue a policy." Rules engines can be part of a larger automated application or provide recommendations to users who need to make a particular type of decision. Fair Isaac, ILOG, Inc., and Pegasystems, Inc. are some of the major providers of rule engines for businesses.

Data mining tools draw on techniques ranging from straightforward arithmetic computation to artificial intelligence, statistics, decision trees, neural networks, and Bayesian network theory. Their objective is to identify patterns in complex and ill-defined data sets. Sprint, for example, uses neural analytical technology to predict which customers are likely to switch wireless carriers and take their existing phone numbers with them. SAS offers both data and text mining capabilities and is a major vendor in both categories.

Text mining tools can help managers quickly identify emerging trends in near–real time. Spiders, or *data crawlers*, which identify and count words and phrases on Web sites, are a simple example of text mining. Text mining tools can be invaluable in sniffing out new trends or relationships. For example, by monitoring technical-user blogs, a vendor can recognize that a new product has a defect within hours of being shipped instead of waiting for complaints to arrive from customers. Other text mining products can recognize references to people, places, things, or topics and use this information to draw inferences about competitor behavior.

Simulation tools model business processes with a set of symbolic, mathematical, scientific, engineering, and financial functions. Much as computer-aided design (CAD) systems are used by engineers to model the design of a new product, simulation tools are used in engineering, R&D, and a surprising number of other applications. For example, simulations can be used as a training device to help users understand the implications of a change to a business process. They can also be used to help streamline the flow of information or products—for example, they can help employees of health care organizations decide where to send donated organs according to criteria ranging from blood type to geographic limitations.

Emerging Analytical Technologies

These are some of the leading-edge technologies that will play a role in analytical applications over the next few years:

Text categorization is the process of using statistical models or rules to rate a document's relevance to a certain topic. For example, text categorization can be used to dynamically evaluate competitors' product assortments on their Web sites.

Genetic algorithms are a class of stochastic optimization methods that use principles found in natural genetic reproduction (crossover or mutations of DNA structures). One common application is to optimize delivery routes.

Expert systems are not a new technology but one that is finally coming of age. Specialized artificial intelligence applications are capable of making expertise available to decision makers (imagine a "Warren Buffett in a box" that gives advice on investment decisions in changing market conditions).

Audio and video mining are much like text or data mining tools, but looking for patterns in audio or images, particularly full-motion images and sound.

Swarm intelligence, as observed in the complex societies of ants and bees, is technology used to increase the realism of simulations and to understand how low-level changes in a system can have dramatic effects.

Information extraction culls and tags concepts such as names, geographical entities, and relationships from largely unstructured (usually) textual data.

Presentation Tools and Applications

Since an analysis is only valuable if it is acted upon, analytic competitors must empower their people to impart their insights to others through reporting tools, scorecards, and portals. Presentation tools should allow users to create ad hoc reports, to interactively visualize complex data, to be alerted to exceptions through a variety of communication tools (such as e-mail, PDAs, or pagers), and to collaboratively share data. (Business intelligence vendors such as Business Objects, Cognos, SAS, and Hyperion Solutions Corporation sell product suites that include data presentation and reporting solutions. As enterprise systems become more analytical, vendors such as SAP and Oracle are rapidly incorporating these capabilities as well.) Commercially purchased analytical applications usually have an interface to be used by information workers, managers, and analysts. But for proprietary analyses, the presentation tools determine how different classes of individuals can use the data. For example, a statistician could directly access a statistical model, but most managers would hesitate to do so.

A new generation of visual analytical tools—from new vendors such as Spotfire and Visual Sciences and from traditional analytics providers such as SAS—allow the manipulation of data and analyses through an intuitive visual interface. A manager, for example, could look at a plot of data, exclude outlier values, and compute a regression line that fits the data—all without any statistical skills. Because they permit exploration of the data without the risk of accidentally modifying the underlying model, visual analytics tools increase the population of users who can employ sophisticated analyses. At Vertex Pharmaceuticals, for example, CIO Steve Schmidt estimates that only 5 percent of his users can make effective use of algorithmic tools, but another 15 percent can manipulate visual analytics.

Operational Processes

This element of the BI architecture answers questions about how the organization creates, manages, and maintains data and applications. It details how a standard set of approved tools and technologies are used to ensure the reliability, scalability, and security of the IT environment. Standards, policies, and processes must also be defined and enforced across the entire organization.

Issues such as privacy and security as well as the ability to archive and audit the data are of critical importance to ensure the integrity of the data. This is a business as well as a technical concern, because lapses in privacy and security (for example, if customer credit card data is stolen) can have dire consequences. One consequence of evolving regulatory and legal requirements is that executives can be found criminally negligent if they fail to establish procedures to document and demonstrate the validity of data used for business decisions.

Conclusion

For most organizations, an enterprise-wide approach to managing data and analytics will be a major departure from current practice. Top management can help the IT architecture team plan a robust technical environment by establishing guiding principles for analytical architecture. Those principles can help to ensure that architectural decisions are aligned with business strategy, corporate culture, and management style.[14] To make that happen, senior management must be committed to the process. Working with IT, senior managers must establish and rigorously enforce comprehensive data management policies, including data standards and consistency in data definitions. They must be committed to the creation and use of high-quality data that is scalable, integrated, well documented, consistent, and standards based. And they must emphasize that the business intelligence architecture should be flexible and able to adapt to changing business needs and objectives. A rigid architecture won't serve the needs of the business in a fast-changing environment.

9

THE FUTURE OF ANALYTICAL COMPETITION

Approaches Driven by Technology, Human
Factors, and Business Strategy

THROUGHOUT THIS BOOK, WE have largely described the present state of analytical competition. In many cases, the analytical competitors we have identified are ahead of their industries in sophistication and progressive practices and are hence bellwethers leading their peers into the future. In this concluding chapter, we speculate broadly on what analytical competitors of the future will be doing differently.

As William Gibson once noted, the future is already here but unevenly distributed. We've already observed leading companies beginning to adopt the approaches described later in the chapter, and we believe they'll simply become more common and more refined. Like most prognosticators of the future, we predict more of what we are writing about: more companies choosing to compete on analytics as their distinctive capability, more companies learning from these analytical competitors to become more analytical themselves, and analytical firms employing analytics in more parts of their businesses. In other cases, we don't know of anybody using a particular practice yet, but logic and trends would dictate that the approach will be employed before long.

We hesitate to be pinned down as to when these elements of the future will transpire, but we estimate that five years is the approximate horizon for when many of these ideas will come to fruition. It's possible that things could accelerate at a faster rate than we predict if the world discovers analytical competition. In the past thirty or so years, however, actual advances in the use of business intelligence, decision support, or whatever the *au courant* term has been, have been relatively slow.

We divide the analytical world of the future into three categories: approaches driven by technology, those involving human capabilities, and those involving changes in business strategy. Technology probably changes the most quickly of these three domains and often forces changes in the other areas.

Technology-Driven Changes

A series of technological capabilities are already used on a small scale within organizations, and we expect they will only expand in the near future. These extrapolations of existing practice include:

- **Pervasive BI software.** We expect that the ability to analyze and report on data will be very common from a software standpoint. Vendors such as Microsoft are already planning to embed analytical capabilities in business versions of Microsoft Office. Smaller companies that can't afford expensive business intelligence software packages will have available free or inexpensive "open source" tools—though we believe that the most advanced capabilities will continue to be expensive.

- **Increasing use of dedicated "business intelligence appliances"** from such vendors as Teradata and Netezza, which are optimized for business intelligence applications and large amounts of data. These are effectively supercomputers that make chewing through large databases and analyses much faster.

- **More automated decisions**, as opposed to relying on humans to look at data and make decisions. This approach has been called *operational business intelligence*, since automated decisions are typically embedded within operational business processes. It might also be called *real-time business intelligence*, since most automated decisions are made immediately.

- **Consistent with the preceding trend**, more real-time (or at least "right-time") analytics. It has historically taken some time—

from days to weeks—for firms to extract data from transaction systems, load it into analytical applications, and make sense of it through analysis. Increasingly, however, managers need to make more rapid decisions, and firms are attempting to implement analytics in real time for at least some decisions.

BostonCoach, a global executive ground transportation company, recently implemented a fleet optimization application to make real-time decisions on the deployment of its vehicles. This application considers up-to-the-minute changes in a range of factors, from traffic patterns to weather-related issues, enabling BostonCoach to live up to its on-time guarantee for passengers. As a result, BostonCoach has increased the optimization of its fleet by upwards of 20 percent while driving down costs along the way.

Most organizations should adopt a *right-time* approach, in which the decision time frame for a class of decisions is determined within an organization, and the necessary data and analytical processes are put in place to deliver it by that time. In a recent *Information Week* survey, 59 percent of the IT executive respondents said they were trying to support real-time business information.[1]

- **Greater use of alerts** to preserve management attention. It has often been assumed that managers would review data and analyses to determine whether key indicators are within desired ranges. However, most managers don't have the time to spend on this activity. More organizations are beginning to make use of automated alerts to notify managers when key indicators are at undesirable levels. Intel, for example, uses alerts to let supply chain commodity managers know when they should act on purchasing and pricing data.[2]

- **More visual analytics**, as opposed to numbers and programming languages. We described this trend in chapter 8, but since it's a very likely aspect of our analytical futures, we're mentioning it again here. As a recent *Wall Street Journal* article put it:

  A new breed of "visual analytics" software aims to make it easier than ever to decipher all that information. The software takes data from multiple sources—including databases and spreadsheets—and creates simple visual representations, such as charts, graphs and maps. They're easier to grasp than pages of data, and they are much more flexible than regular charts and graphs. With just a few clicks, you can manipulate the pictures, checking out the effect of different variables or testing alternative scenarios.[3]

- **More prediction and less reporting.** It's obviously more useful to predict what's going to happen than to explain what's already happened. Prediction, however, generally requires more sophisticated analysis and data than reporting or explanation. Nevertheless, predictive analytics are extending into more and more business domains—from predicting the behavior of customers to predicting the behavior of stocks.

- **More mining of text.** The mining or detailed analysis of data is by now quite advanced, but the mining of text is clearly in its early stages and is likely to expand considerably over the next few years. In chapter 4, we described an example of text mining of automobile service reports at Honda, which supports its distinctive capability of quality manufacturing and service. Other text mining applications could be equally important in analyzing strategic and market trends. The vast amount of textual information on the Internet will undoubtedly fuel a rapid rise for text mining.

There are also a few technology-oriented changes in the world of analytical competition that are not generally present today, even among the most sophisticated firms. However, logic and business needs would suggest that they will become at least somewhat prevalent over the next few years. One is what might be called "direct discovery" by business intelligence applications.[4] Again, tradition dictates that managers drill down to find out what's leading to anomalous results. Most managers, however, have neither the time nor the skill to do a lot of drilling and exploring in data. *Direct discovery* technologies would let managers go directly to the cause of variances in results or performance. This would be a form of predictive analytics, since it would employ a model of how the business is supposed to perform, and would pinpoint factors that are out of range in the causal model of business performance.

The other major advance lies at the opposite end of the analytical process and involves the capture of learning from organizational experiments. In cultures with a broad-scale test-and-learn orientation (and many of our research sites had them, including Google, Amazon.com, Netflix, Harrah's, and Capital One), there is likely to be much greater learning than it would be possible for human beings to absorb. For example, Capital One managers often claim that the company does more than sixty thousand experiments a year. If you're the analyst whose job it is to design a new credit card offering, how can you possibly internalize and act on the results of all those experiments?

The answer, of course, is that you can't. Capital One had a repository of findings from its many experiments, but it was extremely unwieldy for users to search through and learn from. What the company decided to do, then, was to take a just-in-time approach to providing experimental knowledge to its analysts. The company is building a system to guide the analyst through the process of designing a new credit card offering for a specified class of customers. It uses knowledge from the company's experiments to make suggestions at each stage of the design process about what options might work best. It might suggest everything from the optimal interest rate for balance transfers to the best color for the envelope to be used in the direct mail offer to the customer. We have seen such systems used previously in situations where there is simply too much knowledge for a human being to remember—for example, health care order entry and tax processing systems.[5] We expect to see more in environments where test-and-learn cultures create too much experimental learning for people to comprehend.

Human-Driven Changes

While humans don't change as rapidly as information technologies, there are changes in analytical competition that will be driven by the capabilities and configurations of analytical people within organizations. We expect, first of all, that the growth of analytical competition will lead to a need for substantially greater numbers of analytically oriented people—some number of professionals and a much larger group of "analytical amateurs," as we have called them. If many more decisions are to be made based on detailed analysis, many more people will have to have some understanding of how those analyses were performed and when they should be overridden. In short, business intelligence will be increasingly extended to the frontline analytical amateurs within organizations.

From where will these frontline analysts come? Some of these, we believe, will come from business schools, which have always offered some courses in statistics and data analysis. The analytical competitors that do exist are usually led by analytically oriented business school graduates (or professors, in a few cases), but we need more graduates and more intense, cross-functional training. Many schools offer courses in operations or marketing research, but there are a wide variety of other analytical applications that they could and should adopt. We expect that perceptive business schools and their students will focus more on analytical training in the future. Corporations may also need to offer internal programs to educate their people on various forms of analytics.

Of course, not all frontline workers will need to be involved in all analytical activities. It is likely that analytical professionals will have to become expert not only in quantitative analysis but also in job and process design for frontline analysts. They may also have to design information environments for frontline workers that provide just enough analytics and information for them to perform their jobs effectively. As one analyst (who refers to the concept as "pervasive business intelligence") put it, "Pervasive business intelligence is BI for the rest of the organization. It's the ability to take relevant information that is usually reported up to management and push it down to users. At the various organizational levels, the data is presented so that people see only what is most relevant to their day-to-day tasks . . . with expectations and performance clearly identified."[6]

We also expect substantially increased use of outsourced and offshore analytical resources. We noted in chapter 7 that it's difficult to establish the close, trusting relationships between analysts and executives that are necessary for widespread analytical decision making. However, there are certainly analytical tasks that can be accomplished without close interactions with executives. Back-office development and refinement of algorithms, cleaning and integration of data, and the design of small-scale experiments can often be done remotely. Substantial numbers of analytically trained workers in India, Russia, and China will undoubtedly be doing more analytical work in the future. Offshore companies in the outsourcing business are beginning to specialize in such services.

We also anticipate that increasing numbers of firms will develop strong analytical capabilities within their IT organizations. We've already described a Gartner survey in early 2006 finding that business intelligence was the number-one technology priority of corporations.[7] As we have also pointed out in previous chapters, "better management decision making" is the number-one objective of large companies that have installed enterprise resource planning systems. With these priorities and objectives, it's only natural that CIOs and other IT executives will want to increase the IT function's ability to support analytics. This means that they'll be hiring quantitative analysts, specialists in business intelligence software, and IT professionals with expertise in data warehouses and marts. The business functions that IT supports—logistics and supply chain management, marketing, and even HR—will also be hiring analytical experts with a strong IT orientation. It will become increasingly difficult to distinguish analytical people in IT from those in the rest of the business. If you're trying to decide on a technical specialization, business intelligence and analytics are a good bet.

With the rise of analytical people across the entire organization, we can expect a greater need for structure and guidance in the management of their activities. As we've noted earlier, there will be no shortage of analytical tools, whether they're spreadsheets, visual analytical systems, or some other form of software. However, if corporate strategies depend on the results of analytics, they have to be done with accuracy and professionalism.

How will companies provide greater structure and human capability for strategically important analyses? There will be no single method but rather a variety of tools and approaches. One way is to have the software guide the analysis process, as we've described in chapter 7. Analytical software applications can guide an analyst through a decision process, either making the decision itself (perhaps with a human override option) or ensuring that a human decision maker has all needed information and isn't violating any important statistical assumptions. Another answer would be substantial education. We believe that most organizations would benefit from education to create more capable analysts and improve the skills of existing ones. A third would be a group of "coaches" to help amateur analysts and certify their work as well done. For analytical work that substantially affects financial performance, internal and external auditors may need to get involved. Whatever the means, companies will need to both build analytical capability in their employees and ensure that they're doing a good job. As we've already described, some leading companies are beginning to employ these approaches for building human analytical capability through some sort of business intelligence competency center.

This attention to human analytical prowess won't stop at the analysis stage. Firms will also want to improve and better understand how key decisions are made. The best information and analytics aren't very useful unless good decisions are made and the right actions taken. Therefore, we expect that many organizations will begin to formally manage their decision-making processes, which has largely been treated as a black box thus far. They will educate managers on analytical decision-making processes, review their key decisions with regard to the process used, and evaluate them on not only the outcome of their decisions but also the processes, information, and analyses used to make them. We've already begun to hear of some companies taking this focus. Intel offers a series of educational programs on managerial decision making, and executives at Quaker Chemical have focused on how information and analytics are used in decision making.

Strategy-Driven Changes

We anticipate that a number of changes in the analytical environment will be driven by business strategies. As more firms become aware of the possibilities for analytical competition, they will push the boundaries of analytics in their products, services, and business models. Virtually every provider of data and information services, for example, will probably offer analytics to its customers as a value-added service. Data itself has become something of a commodity, and customers for data often can't find the time or people to analyze it themselves.

We also expect to see more analytics embedded in or augmenting products and services—describing, for example, the optimum way to make use of those offerings within the customer's business processes. The golf club we described in chapter 3 that tells you how well you are swinging it is a good example. We also expect to see automobiles (or insurance companies) that analyze how safely you are driving, health care providers that analyze how healthily you are eating and living, and industrial machinery that tells you how well you are using it. Of course, we may tire of all this advice.

This trend will be only a part of a broader one involving supplying analytics to customers and suppliers. We've already mentioned some firms that give analytical information to their customers. There are others we haven't mentioned that are beginning to do this to some degree. Marriott, for example, is beginning to share more analytical information with both channel partners—online and traditional travel agencies, for example—and major corporate customers. Channel partners get analyses involving pricing, joint promotions, and inventory; customers receive data and analysis that helps them with their own travel management. We expect that most firms will begin to view the internal audience for analytics and business intelligence as only one of several potential recipients, and that relationships with suppliers and customers will increasingly include the provision of analytics.

Another strategic trend involves the content of analytics. Thus far, most quantitative analyses are about relatively tangible entities: inventory units, dollars, customers, and so forth. Most organizations realize, however, that intangible assets and capabilities are extremely important in their competitive success. For more than a decade, there have been arguments in favor of measuring and managing intangibles, which include such factors as human capital, intellectual capital, brand, R&D capability, and other nonfinancial assets. Numerous articles and books have been written on the subject, and there is a consensus that intangible assets are important to both company success and external perceptions of company value. In an Accenture/Economist Intelligence Unit survey, for example, "today's senior executives see managing intangible assets as a major issue. Fully 94 percent consider the comprehensive management of intangible assets important; 50 percent consider it one of the top three management issues facing their company."[8]

Someday, perhaps, intangible assets will be reported upon by companies as a part of their regular financial reporting processes, and they may be forced to create and report on analytics involving intangibles. This has also been advocated by Robert Kaplan and David Norton of Balanced Scorecard fame.[9] There is no need to wait until such reporting is mandated by regulation, however. In the near future, we believe, companies will begin to take steps today to analyze and report intangible assets. If there is enhanced value and competitiveness in managing intangibles, there is no reason why executives can't begin to make decisions and take actions based on intangible assets and capabilities now.

Technology could play a substantial (but not exclusive) role in generating and analyzing intangible capabilities.[10] Intangibles are not easily reducible to a set of numbers, and hence this type of analysis will often involve work with text and other less structured forms of information. We've already described, for example, how Honda uses text mining to identify and head off potential quality problems in its cars.

184 • BUILDING AN ANALYTICAL CAPABILITY

Similar text and Web mining approaches could be used to, for example, better understand customer perceptions of service and brand value. Consultant and former academic Richard Hackathorn was writing as early as 1999 that "the web is the mother of all data warehouses," and even then described a Web farming application for Eaton Corporation that was "monitoring hundreds of markets for technology shifts, emerging competitors, and governmental regulations."[11] What could be more strategic and competitive? This has not been an area that even analytical competitors have explored much, but it should be going forward. It is high time for firms to begin exploiting the online text world's potential for assessing intangibles.

Finally, we expect that strategic concerns will also drive firms to pay substantial attention to new metrics and their interrelationships in analyses and scorecards. We heard from a number of analytical competitors that they start with metrics in thinking about applying analysis to a distinctive capability. They either invent a new metric from their own proprietary data or refine an existing one. As metrics become commonplace (e.g., as we have discussed, the FICO score in consumer credit or the batting average in baseball), companies and organizations go beyond them to new measurement frontiers. We anticipate particularly high levels of activity in the domain of human resources and talent management, since these have been relatively unmeasured in the past.

Once developed, of course, metrics must be incorporated into established scorecards and measurement processes, and the relationships between different measures must be explored and understood. Most importantly, these metrics must be incorporated into business and management decision-making processes. Just developing a measure, and just using it in some analyses, is never enough.

The Future of Analytical Competition

We'll end this book by discussing broadly what will happen to analytical competitors in the future. This will serve as both a summary of the key attributes of analytical competitors and a prediction of the future, because analytical competitors will continue to do more of what made them successful in the first place.

Analytical competitors will continue to examine their strategies and their business capabilities to understand where they can get an analytical edge. They'll focus on what makes their organizations distinctive and how analytics can support or drive a distinctive capability. Analytics will eventually be applied to most areas of their business—their motto will be, "If it's worth doing, it's worth doing analytically." These companies will identify measures of the distinctive capability that other organizations don't yet employ. After they identify a measure, they'll collect data on it and embed decisions based on the measures into their daily work processes.

In order to continue refining their analytical capabilities, companies will focus on both their human and technological dimensions. On the human side, they'll try to further embed an analytical orientation into the culture and to test as many hypotheses as they can. Their executives will argue for analytical strategies and decisions with passion and personal example. Their managers will constantly press subordinates for data or analytics before they take major actions.

The managers of analytical competitors of the future will not be narrow "quant jocks." They'll always be thinking broadly about whether their analytical models and data are still relevant to their businesses. If a particular type of analysis becomes commoditized throughout their industries, they'll find some new basis for analytical competition. They'll use intuition sparingly but strategically when it isn't possible to test an assertion or gather data for an analysis. They'll undoubtedly be hotly pursued by other firms that also want to be analytical competitors. Fortunately for their employers, they'll find their jobs stimulating and satisfying and will stay put as long as they're recognized and promoted.

There will be continue to be people in these organizations whose job primarily involves developing and refining analytics—analytical professionals. They will either work in a central group or be highly networked, and they'll share approaches and ideas. They will also work to educate the analytical amateurs of the organizations, who need to understand how analytical models and tools support them in their jobs. The analytical competitor of the future will also supplement internal analytical resources with outsourced or offshore expertise.

Analytical competitors will continue to have lots of data that is generated from enterprise systems, point-of-sale systems, and Web transactions, as well as external data from customers and suppliers. They'll organize it and put it aside for analysis in warehouses. They will ensure that data is integrated and common in the areas of their business where it really matters. They'll have integrated business intelligence suites or "platforms" that support reporting and analytics. In domains where decisions must be made very rapidly or very often, they'll embed analysis into automated decision systems, allowing human overrides only under specified conditions.

Perhaps most importantly, analytical competitors will continue to find ways to outperform their competitors. They'll get the best customers and charge them exactly the price that the customer is willing to pay for their product and service. They'll have the most efficient and effective marketing campaigns and promotions. Their customer service will excel, and their customers will be loyal in return. Their supply chains will be ultraefficient, and they'll have neither excess inventory nor stock-outs. They'll have the best people or the best players in the industry, and the employees will be evaluated and compensated based on their specific contributions. They'll understand what nonfinancial processes and factors drive their financial performance, and they'll be able to predict and diagnose problems before they become too problematic. They will make a lot of money, win a lot of games, or help solve the world's most pressing problems. They will continue to lead us into the future.

Notes

Chapter 1

1. Netflix quotation from Jena McGregor, "At Netflix, the Secret Sauce Is Software," *Fast Company*, October 2005, 50. Other Netflix information comes from the company Web site (http://www.netflix.com); Mark Hall, "Web Analytics Get Real," *Computerworld*, April 1, 2002; Timothy J. Mullaney, "Netflix: The Mail-Order Movie House That Clobbered Blockbuster," *BusinessWeek Online*, May 25, 2006, http://www.businessweek.com/smallbiz/content/may2006/sb20060525_268860.htm?campaign_id=search; and a telephone interview with chief product officer Neil Hunt on July 7, 2006.

2. The "long tail" concept has been popularized by Chris Anderson in *The Long Tail: Why the Future of Business Is Selling Less of More* (New York: Hyperion, 2006).

3. We define *distinctive capabilities* as the integrated business processes and capabilities that together serve customers in ways that are differentiated from competitors and that create an organization's formula for business success.

4. David Darlington, "The Chemistry of a 90+ Wine," *New York Times Sunday Magazine*, August 7, 2005.

5. Thomas H. Davenport, "Competing on Analytics," *Harvard Business Review*, January 2006; Thomas H. Davenport, "Analyze This," *CIO*, October 1, 2005, http://www.cio.com/archive/100105/comp_advantage.html; and Thomas H. Davenport and Jeanne G. Harris, "Automated Decision Making Comes of Age," *MIT Sloan Management Review*, Summer 2005.

6. One of the first books written on the subject of decision support was by Peter G. W. Keen and Michael S. Scott Morton, *Decision Support Systems: An Organizational Perspective* (Reading, MA: Addison-Wesley, 1978). A subsequent book written on the topic is by John W. Rockart and David W.

De Long, *Executive Support Systems: The Emergence of Top Management Computer Use* (Homewood, IL: Dow Jones-Irwin, 1988). Also note Tom Gerrity Jr.'s 1971 article, "The Design of Man-Machine Decision Systems: An Application to Portfolio Management," *MIT Sloan Management Review* 12, no. 2, (1971): 59–75; and Charles Stabell's 1974 work, "On the Development of Decision Support Systems on a Marketing Problem," *Information Processing*, as formative research in the field of DSS.

7. Rockart and De Long, *Executive Support Systems.*

8. Described in "Business Intelligence Software Market to Reach $3 Billion by 2009," *CRM Today*, February 8, 2006, http://www.crm2day.com/news/crm/117297.php.

9. For example, refer to Jeffrey Pfeffer and Robert Sutton's article "Evidence-Based Management," *Harvard Business Review*, January 2006; and Eric Bonabeau's article "Don't Trust Your Gut," *Harvard Business Review*, May 2003.

10. Malcolm Gladwell, *Blink: The Power of Thinking Without Thinking* (New York: Little, Brown, 2005).

11. Gary Klein, *Sources of Power: How People Make Decisions* (Cambridge, MA: MIT Press, 1999).

12. Alan Deutschman, "Inside the Mind of Jeff Bezos," *Fast Company*, August 2004, 52.

13. Michael Lewis, *Moneyball: The Art of Winning an Unfair Game* (New York: W. W. Norton & Company, 2004).

14. Alan Schwartz, *The Numbers Game: Baseball's Lifelong Fascination with Statistics* (New York: St. Martin's Griffin, 2005).

15. Russell Adams, "The Culture of Winning: Atlanta Braves Have Secured 14 Straight Division Titles, and Team's GM Tells Why," *Wall Street Journal*, October 5, 2005.

16. Buzz Bissinger, *Three Nights in August* (Boston: Houghton Mifflin, 2005), 201.

17. Andy Wasynczuk, then chief operating officer, New England Patriots, telephone interview with Tom Davenport, January 11, 2005.

18. From "Interview with Packers Director of Research and Development Mike Eayrs," *Football Outsiders*, June 22, 2004, http://www.football-outsiders.com/ramblings.php?p=226&cat=8.

19. Chris Ballard, "Measure of Success," *Sports Illustrated*, October 24, 2005.

Chapter 2

1. Professor Mark Oleson of the University of Missouri, quoted in Pat Curry, "The Future of FICO," Bankrate.com, November 1, 2005, http://www.bankrate.com/smrtpg/news/debt/debtcreditguide/fico-future1.asp.

2. Rajiv Lal and Patricia Matrone Carrolo, "Harrah's Entertainment, Inc.," Case 9-502-011 (Boston: Harvard Business School, 2002), 6.

3. Data from a BetterManagement survey and described in Gloria J. Miller, Dagmar Brautigam, and Stefanie V. Gerlach, *Business Intelligence Competency Centers: A Team Approach to Maximizing Competitive Advantage* (Hoboken, NJ: Wiley, 2006).

4. For more information on spreadsheet errors, see Raymond Panko's article, "What We Know About Spreadsheet Errors," *Journal of End User Computing* 10, no. 2 (Spring 1998): 15–21.

5. Definition of BICC from a SAS Web site, http://www.sas.com/consult/bicc.html.

6. Christopher H. Paige, "Capital One Financial Corporation," Case 9-700-124 (Boston: Harvard Business School, 2001).

7. Victoria Chang and Jeffrey Pfeffer, "Gary Loveman and Harrah's Entertainment," Case OB45 (Stanford, CA: Stanford Graduate School of Business, November 2003), 7.

8. Keith Coulter, managing director, U.K. cards and loans, Barclay, telephone interview with Tom Davenport, October 11, 2005.

9. Barry C. Smith, Dirk P. Gunther, B. Venkateshwara Rao, and Richard M. Ratliff, "E-Commerce and Operations Research in Airline Planning, Marketing, and Distribution," *Interfaces*, March–April 2001, 37–55.

10. Tallys H. Yunes, Dominic Napolitano, et al., "Building Efficient Product Portfolios at John Deere," working paper, Carnegie Mellon University, Pittsburgh, PA, April 2004.

11. Gary H. Anthes, "Modeling Magic," *Computerworld*, February 7, 2005.

12. Gary Loveman, CEO of Harrah's, from presentations and interviews with Tom Davenport, January 2005–June 2006.

13. The American Medical Informatics Association defines *informatics* as "the effective organization, analysis, management, and use of information in health care." See http://www.amia.org/informatics/.

Chapter 3

1. Stephanie Overby, "The Price Is Always Right," *CIO*, February 15, 2005.

2. Ibid.

3. Joanne Kelley, "Risky Business," *Context*, July-August 1999.

4. See http://www.progressive.com.

5. Jim Collins, *Good to Great: Why Some Companies Make the Leap . . . and Others Don't* (New York: HarperCollins, 2001), 69.

6. Henry Morris, Stephen Graham, Per Andersen, Karen Moser, Robert Blumstein, Dan Velssel, Nathaniel Martinez, and Marilyn Carr, *The*

Financial Impact of Business Analytics: Distribution of Results by ROI Category, IDC #28689 (Framingham, MA: International Data Corporation, January 2003).

7. Henry Morris, *Predictive Analytics and ROI: Lessons from IDC's Financial Impact Study*, IDC #30080 (Framingham, MA: International Data Corporation, September 2003).

8. Kendall's tau_b - coefficient: .194, error: .107 (one-tailed test); Spearman's rho - coefficient: .272, error: .094 (one-tailed test). The small sample size of publicly reporting firms (N=20) explains the relatively low significance levels.

9. For this study, we defined an *enterprise system* as an integrated software package (from vendors such as SAP and Oracle) that addresses most of an organization's day-to-day transactional data processing needs.

10. For more details, see Jeanne G. Harris and Thomas H. Davenport, *New Growth from Enterprise Systems* (Wellesley, MA: Accenture Institute for High Performance Business, May 2006).

11. Thomas H. Davenport, Jeanne G. Harris, and Susan Cantrell, *The Return of Enterprise Solutions: The Director's Cut* (Wellesley, MA: Accenture Institute for High Performance Business, 2002).

12. Using Pearson's product-moment coefficient of correlation, profit has a significant positive correlation with analytical orientation at r=.136 (p = .011), revenue growth is significantly correlated at r=.124 (p = .020), and shareholder return is correlated at r=.122 (p = .022).

13. For the purposes of this study, top and low performers were defined by asking respondents to assess their standing—on a scale of 1 to 5—in the industry relative to profit, shareholder return, and revenue growth. Top performers scored 14 or higher (out of a possible 15 points); 13 percent of the sample scored at this level. Low performers scored 8 or fewer points and represented 16 percent of the sample. We found these scores to be highly correlated with publicly reported business performance. We excluded government respondents because government agencies could not be evaluated using these criteria.

14. Progressive Insurance, *Annual Report to Shareholders*, 2005.

15. Michael Lewis in a speech at Accenture, San Francisco, June 16, 2006.

16. CompStat is described in detail on Wikipedia-see http://en.wikipedia.org/wiki/CompStat. Steven Levitt has questioned the crime reductions due to CompStat in "Understanding Why Crime Fell in the 1990s: Four Factors that Explain the Decline and Six That Do Not," *Journal of Economic Perspectives* 18, no. 1 (Winter 2004): 163–190.

17. Cindy Blanthorne and Kristen Selvey Yance, "The Tax Gap: Measuring the IRS's Bottom Line," *CPA Journal Online* (New York State Society

of CPAs), April 2006, http://www.nysscpa.org/cpajournal/2006/406/essentials/p40.htm.

18. Catherine Arnst, "The Best Medical Care in the U.S.," *Business-Week*, July 17, 2006, 51.

19. Vivienne Jupp and Elisabeth Astall, "Technology in Government: Riding the Waves of Change," Accenture Government Executive Series report, 2002, http://www.ebusinessforum.gr/content/downloads/gove_waves.pdf.

20. Eleanor Laise, "Wall Street Pushes Computerized Funds," *Wall Street Journal*, April 7, 2006.

21. See http://www.catalinamarketing.com.

22. Sunil Garga, president of IRI's Analytical Insights group, telephone interview with Jeanne Harris, October 2, 2006.

23. Richard G. Hamermesh, Michael J. Roberts, and Taz Pirmohamed, "ProfitLogic," Case 9-802-110 (Boston: Harvard Business School, 2003), 7.

24. David Berlind, "Golf Analytics: Meet Clients at a Virtual Course While Improving Your Swing," *Between the Lines*, ZDNet blog, September 29, 2005, http://blogs.zdnet.com/BTL/?p=1941.

Chapter 4

1. For more on enterprise performance management and the use of analytics, see: Michael R. Sutcliff and Michael A. Donnellan, *CFO Insights: Delivering High Performance* (Chichester, UK: John Wiley & Sons, 2006), Chapter 5, "Enterprise Performance Management."

2. Jerry Z. Shan et al., "Dynamic Modeling and Forecasting on Enterprise Revenue with Derived Granularities," Hewlett-Packard Laboratories, May 2005, http://www.hpl.hp.com/techreports/2005/HPL-2005-90.pdf.

3. Ibid., 6.

4. David Larcker and Chris Ittner, "Coming Up Short on Nonfinancial Measurement," *Harvard Business Review*, November 2003.

5. Mark Leon, "Ad Game Analytics," *Intelligent Enterprise*, January 21, 2005.

6. John Ballow, Robert Thomas, and Goran Roos, "Future Value: The $7 Trillion Challenge," *Accenture Outlook*, no. 1, 2004, http://www.accenture.com/xd/xd.asp?it=enweb&xd=ideas\outlook\1_2004\manage.xml.

7. For example, see Peter D. Easton, Travis S. Harris, and James A. Ohlson, "Aggregate Accounting Returns Can Explain Most of Security Returns," *Journal of Accounting and Economics* (1992); Gary C. Biddle, Robert M. Bowen, and James S. Wallace, "Does EVA(c) Beat Earnings? Evidence on Associations with Stock Returns and Firm Values," *Journal of Accounting and Economics* (1997); and Stephen O'Byrne, "EVA and Its Critics," *Journal of Applied Corporate Finance* (1997).

8. Ballow, Thomas, and Roos, "Future Value."

9. John Nolan of MCI, telephone interview with Tom Davenport, February 18, 2005.

10. Quotation from V. C. Narayanan, "Customer Profitability and Customer Relationship Management at RBC Financial Group (Abridged)," Case 9-102-072 (Boston: Harvard Business School, revised November 13, 2002), 7. Other information about RBC from Kevin Purkiss, telephone interview with Tom Davenport, December 16, 2005.

11. Narayanan, "Customer Profitability and Customer Relationship Management at RBC," 15–16.

12. Purkiss, interview.

13. Shigeru Komatsu of Toshiba Semiconductor, interview with Tom Davenport, April 10, 2006.

14. Spotfire, Inc., "Toshiba Uses Visual, Interactive Analytics from Spotfire to Gain an Information Advantage in High Tech Manufacturing," news release, November 28, 2005, http://www.spotfire.com.

15. Tallys H. Yunes, Dominic Napolitano, et al., "Building Efficient Product Portfolios at John Deere," working paper, Carnegie Mellon University, Pittsburgh, PA, April 2004.

16. Bill Brougher, interview with Tom Davenport, July 18, 2006.

17. Barry Werth, *The Billion Dollar Molecule: One Company's Quest for the Perfect Drug* (New York: Simon & Schuster, 1995), 135.

18. Steven Schmidt of Vertex Pharmaceuticals, interview with Tom Davenport, April 5, 2006.

19. Alex Bangs, "Predictive Biosimulation and Virtual Patients in Pharmaceutical R&D," in *Medicine Meets Virtual Reality 13: The Magical Next Becomes the Medical Now*, eds. James D. Westwood et al., vol. 111, Studies in Health Technology and Informatics (Amsterdam, Netherlands: IOS Press, 2005), 41.

20. Stefan Thomke, "R&D Comes to Services: Bank of America's Pathbreaking Experiments," *Harvard Business Review*, April 2003.

21. Information about American Healthways obtained from a presentation by Dr. Carter Coberly at the Health Information Technology Summit, Washington, DC, 2004, http://www.ehcca.com/presentations/cahealthit2/2_03_1.pdf.

22. Thomas H. Davenport and John Glaser, "Just in Time Comes to Knowledge Management," *Harvard Business Review*, July 2002.

23. Bill Belichick, "Quotes from New England Patriots Media Day," February 1, 2005, cited in James Lavin, *Management Secrets of the New England Patriots*, vol. 2 (Stamford, CT: Pointer Press, 2005), 159.

24. Quotation from Michelle Thompson, Asia Pacific vice president for HR at American Express, in "Mastering HR Analytics with Technology," *Human Resources (Australia)*, March 27, 2006.

25. Joanne Kelly, "Getting All the Credit," Context Magazine, online at: http://www.contextmag.com/setFrameRedirect.asp?src=/archives/200202/Feature2GettingalltheCredit.asp.

Chapter 5

1. In our survey of about four hundred organizations with enterprise systems, there was a relationship between analytics and supply chain integration. The correlation (Pearson product-moment correlation, one-tailed test) between strong analytical orientation and integration with suppliers was .23.

2. Tony Kontzer, "Big Bet On Customer Loyalty," *InformationWeek,* February 9, 2004.

3. American Customer Satisfaction Index, University of Michigan, 2005, fourth-quarter rankings, updated February 21, 2006, http://www.theacsi.org/fourth_quarter.htm.

4. Aaron O. Patrick, "Econometrics Buzzes Ad World as a Way of Measuring Results," *Wall Street Journal*, August 16, 2005.

5. Mark Leon, "Ad Game Analytics," *Intelligent Enterprise*, January 21, 2005.

6. Jim Ericson, "Coming to Account," *Business Intelligence Review*, April 2005.

7. Clive Humby and Terry Hunt, *Scoring Points: How Tesco is Winning Customer Loyalty* (Philadelphia: Kogan Page, Ltd., 2003).

8. Yankee Group research report from 2005, quoted in Gary Anthes, "The Price Point," *Computerworld*, July 24, 2006, 34.

9. Scott Friend, "Changing the Game: New Strategies for Merchandising Innovation" (presentation at the National Retail Foundation conference, January 16, 2005, http://www.nrf.com/Attachments.asp?id=6991), which cites *Retail Info Systems News*, October 2004.

10. Deena Cherenze, "Pricing and Sales Effectiveness Arm the Front Line" (Yankee Group, February 2006).

11. Marcel Corstjens and Jeffrey Merrihue, "Optimal Marketing," *Harvard Business Review*, October 2003.

12. Kevin Kelleher, "66,207,896 Bottles of Beer on the Wall-Anheuser-Busch's Top-Secret Data Network Tracks Inventory," *Business 2.0*, CNNMoney.com, February 25, 2004.

13. Best Buy annual report, 2005.

14. Ibid.

15. Matthew Boyle, "Best Buy's Giant Gamble," *Fortune*, April 3, 2006.

16. "Which Customers Are Worth Keeping and Which Ones Aren't? Managerial Uses of CLV," *Knowledge@Wharton*, July 30, 2003, http://www.whartonsp.com/articles/article.asp?p=328189&rl=1.

17. Peggy Anne Salz, "High Performance—Intelligent Use of Information is a Powerful Corporate Tool," *Wall Street Journal*, April 27, 2006.

18. Pankaj Ghemawat, Stephen P. Bradley, and Ken Mark, "Wal-Mart Stores in 2003," Case 9-704-430 (Boston: Harvard Business School, September 2003).

19. Figures on Wal-Mart are from a presentation given by chief information officer Linda Dillman, quoted by Dan Briody in *BizBytes*, April 2006.

20. Len Kennedy, vice president of UPS, in "What Can Brown Do for You?" *Location Intelligence*, December 5, 2002.

21. Taken from 1954 UPS annual report.

22. Beth Bacheldor, "Breakthrough," *InformationWeek*, February 9, 2004, http://www.informationweek.com/industries/showArticle.jhtml?articleID=17602194&pgno=1&queryText=.

23. Norbert Turek, "FedEx and UPS Lead the Logistics Pack," *InformationWeek*, January 11, 2001.

24. Richard Tomkins, "The Art of Keeping Customers Happy," *Financial Times* (London), June 17, 2005.

25. Alejandro Ruelas-Gossi and Donald Sull, "The Art of Innovating on a Shoestring," *Financial Times* (London), September 24, 2004.

26. Rita Gunther McGrath and Ian C. MacMillan, "MarketBusting: Strategies for Exceptional Business Growth," *Harvard Business Review*, March 2005, 80–89.

Chapter 6

1. Barbara Desouer of Bank of America, interview with Jeanne Harris, May 8, 2006.

2. For more on effective decision-making processes, see Jeanne G. Harris, *The Insight-to-Action Loop: Transforming Information into Business Performance* (Wellesley, MA: Accenture Institute for High Performance Business, February 2005), http://www.accenture.com/Global/Research_and_Insights/Institute_For_High_Performance_Business/By_Publication_Type/Research_Notes/InsightToPractice.htm; and Glover Ferguson, Sanjay Mathur, and Baiju Singh, "Evolving from Information to Insight," *MIT Sloan Management Review* 46, no. 2, (2005): 51–58.

3. Vivienne Jupp and Elisabeth Astall, "Technology in Government: Riding the Waves of Change," Accenture Government Executive Series report, 2002, http://www.ebusinessforum.gr/content/downloads/gove_waves.pdf.

4. Mark Twain attributes this quote to Disraeli; see Charles Neider, ed., *The Autobiography of Mark Twain* (New York: HarperCollins, 2000), 195.

5. For more on this topic, see Darrell Huff, *How to Lie with Statistics* (New York: W. W. Norton & Company, 1954).

6. For more on preventing statistical abuse, see "The Use and Misuse of Statistics," *Harvard Management Update* 11, no. 3 (March 2006).

Chapter 7

1. Thomas H. Davenport, Jeanne G. Harris, David W. De Long, and Alvin L. Jacobson, "Data to Knowledge to Results: Building an Analytic Capability," *California Management Review* 43, no. 2, 117–138.

2. For more on evidence-based management, see Jeffrey Pfeffer and Robert I. Sutton, *Hard Facts, Dangerous Half-Truths, and Total Nonsense: Profiting from Evidence-Based Management* (Boston: Harvard Business School Press, 2006).

3. Interview of William Perez by Michael Barbaro, "A Not-so-Nice Nike Divorce Came Down to Data vs. Feel," *The New York Times*, January 28, 2006, National edition, B4.

4. Donald A. Marchand, William J. Kettinger, and John D. Rollins, *Information Orientation: The Link to Business Performance* (New York: Oxford University Press, 2002).

5. Stephen Baker, "Math Will Rock Your World," *BusinessWeek*, January 23, 2006, http://www.businessweek.com/print/magazine/content/06_04/b3968001.htm?chan=gl.

6. Hal Varian, e-mail correspondence with Tom Davenport, December 6, 2005.

7. Ibid.

8. Job listed on Monster.com on July 26, 2006, for McKesson Corporation.

9. Bob Deangelis, telephone interview with Tom Davenport, February 8, 2005.

10. Head of an analytical group at a consumer products firm who wished to remain anonymous, telephone interview with Tom Davenport, May 24, 2005.

11. For more on this topic, see Thomas H. Davenport and Jeanne G. Harris, "Automated Decision Making Comes of Age," *MIT Sloan Management Review*, Summer 2005, 83–89.

12. For a description of business rules technology, see Barbara von Halle, *Business Rules Applied: Building Better Systems Using the Business Rule Approach* (New York: Wiley, 2001).

Chapter 8

1. Julie Gallagher, "Business-Savvy CIO Turns Tech-Savvy CEO," *FinanceTech*, May 31, 2001,http://www.financetech.com/showArticle.jhtml? articleID=14706275.

2. Erick Schonfeld, "The Great Giveaway," *Business 2.0*, CNNMoney. com, April 2005.

3. Hugh Watson, Barbara Wixom, et al., "Real Time Business Intelligence: Best Practices at Continental Airlines," *Information Systems Management* 23, no. 1, (2005): 7-18.

4. M. McDonald and M. Blosch, *Gartner's 2006 EXP CIO Survey* (Stamford, CT: Gartner, Inc., January 2006).

5. Marcia Stepanek, "Q&A with Progressive's Peter Lewis," *BusinessWeek*, September 12, 2000.

6. Charles Babcock, "Data, Data Everywhere," *InformationWeek*, January 9, 2006.

7. International Data Corporation, *Business Analytics Implementation Challenges: Top Ten Considerations for 2003 and Beyond*, IDC Report 28728 (Framingham, MA: International Data Corporation, January 2003).

8. Nicole Haggerty and Darren Meister, "Business Intelligence Strategy at Canadian Tire," Case 903E19 (London, Ontario: Ivey School of Business 2003).

9. Donald Marchand, William Kettinger, and John Rollins, *Making the Invisible Visible: How Companies Win with the Right Information, People and IT* (New York: Wiley, 2001).

10. Madan Sheina, "Refocused: Back to the Future," *Computer Business Review*, September 2005.

11. Henry Morris et al., *The Financial Impact of Business Analytics: Distribution of Results by ROI Category*, IDC #28689 (Framingham, MA: International Data Corporation, January 2003).

12. The Data Warehousing Institute, *Enterprise Business Intelligence: Strategies and Technologies for Deploying BI on an Enterprise Scale* (Renton, WA: The Data Warehousing Institute, August 2005).

13. For more information on spreadsheet errors, see Raymond Panko's paper "What We Know About Spreadsheet Errors," January 2005, http://panko.cba.hawaii.edu/ssr/Mypapers/whatknow.htm.

14. The principles-based approach to IT architecture is described in Thomas H. Davenport, Michael Hammer, and Tauno Metsisto, "How Executives Can Shape Their Company's Information Systems," *Harvard Business Review*, March–April 1989, 130–134.

Chapter 9

1. Data from Outlook 2006 Survey, *Information Week*, January 2, 2006.

2. Charles P. Seeley and Thomas H. Davenport, "Integrating Business Intelligence and Knowledge Management at Intel," *Knowledge Management Review* 8, no. 6 (January–February 2006): 10–15.

3. Michael Totty, "A New Look for Number Crunching," *Wall Street Journal-The Journal Report: Technology*, April 3, 2006.

4. See the article by Don Allen Price, "The Dawn of a New Era: What's Next in Business Intelligence?" *DM Review*, February 2006, http://www.dmreview.com/article_sub.cfm?articleId=1046592.

5. Thomas H. Davenport and John Glaser, "Just-in-Time Comes to Knowledge Management," *Harvard Business Review*, July 2002, 107–111.

6. Dave Mittereder, "Pervasive Business Intelligence: Enhancing Key Performance Indicators," *DM Review*, April 2005, http://www.dmreview.com/article_sub.cfm?articleID=1023894.

7. M. McDonald and M. Blosch, *Gartner's 2006 EXP CIO Survey* (Stamford, CT: Gartner, Inc., January 2006).

8. Accenture, "Intangible Assets and Future Value: An Accenture Study Conducted by the Economist Intelligence Unit," January 2005, http://www.accenture.com/Global/Services/By_Subject/Shareholder_Value/R_and_I/SurveyAssets.htm.

9. Robert S. Kaplan and David P. Norton, "Measuring the Strategic Readiness of Intangible Assets," *Harvard Business Review*, February 2004, 52–63.

10. We addressed this issue in Jeanne G. Harris and Thomas H. Davenport, "The Information Environment for Intangible Asset Management," Accenture Research Note, June 2004, http://www.accenture.com/Global/Research_and_Insights/Institute_For_High_Performance_Business/By_Publication_Type/Research_Notes/TheAssetManagement_old.htm.

11. Richard D. Hackathorn, *Web Farming for the Data Warehouse* (San Francisco: Morgan Kaufmann, 1999), 23.

Index

About the Authors

Tom Davenport is the President's Distinguished Professor in Information Technology and Management at Babson College and Director of Research for Babson Executive Education. He leads sponsored research programs on analytics, knowledge management, process management, and innovation.

Tom wrote, coauthored, or edited eleven other books, including the first books on business process reengineering and achieving value from enterprise systems, and the best seller, *Working Knowledge* (with Larry Prusak), on knowledge management. He has written more than one hundred articles for such publications as *Harvard Business Review*, *MIT Sloan Management Review*, *California Management Review*, the *Financial Times*, and many other publications. Tom has also been a columnist for CIO, *Information Week*, and *Darwin* magazines. In 2003 he was named one of the world's "Top 25 Consultants" by *Consulting* magazine, and in 2005 was named one of the world's top three analysts of business and technology by readers of *Optimize* magazine.

Jeanne G. Harris is director of research and an executive research fellow at Accenture's Institute for High Performance Business where she leads research in the areas of information, technology, and strategy. During her thirty years at Accenture, Harris has consulted to a wide variety of organizations in many different industries worldwide. She has led Accenture's business intelligence, analytics, performance management, knowledge management, and data warehousing consulting practices. She has worked extensively with clients seeking to improve their managerial information, decision-making, analytical, and knowledge management capabilities.

Jeanne earned her master's degree in information science from the University of Illinois and a BA from Washington University in St. Louis. She has authored numerous book chapters and articles in leading management publications, including *MIT Sloan Management Review*, *California Management Review*, and *Optimize*. Her research has been quoted extensively by the international business press, including the *Wall Street Journal*, the *Financial Times*, and *Nihon Keizai Shimbun*.